THE NESTORIAN CHURCHES

THE NESTORIAN CHURCHES

A CONCISE HISTORY OF NESTORIAN
CHRISTIANITY IN ASIA FROM
THE PERSIAN SCHISM
TO THE MODERN
ASSYRIANS

by

AUBREY R. VINE

M.A., B.D., B.Sc.

With Foreword by

HIS BEATITUDE
MAR ESHAI SHIMUN
PATRIARCH OF THE EAST

LONDON:
INDEPENDENT PRESS, LTD
MEMORIAL HALL, E.C.4

First published 1937
All rights reserved

Made *and* printed *in* Great Britain
By The Camelot Press Ltd
London *and* Southampton

TO

PERCY EDWARD BRAND

my Mæcenas

FOREWORD

IF this book serves to stimulate interest in the Church of the East, whose history has been so much more difficult than that of Western Christianity, I shall be gratified. My people have had a great struggle to maintain their Christian faith. They have had to stand against other religions having the advantage of State support, and they have frequently suffered in great racial disturbances. But their witness goes on, and I pray God that easier days may soon be granted them; this work may help toward that end if it enlarges the vision and sympathy of English-speaking Christians. I favour every contribution toward the bringing into closer relationship of all the people of God: for 'there shall be one fold, and one shepherd.'

Eshai Shimun,
By the Grace of God,
Catholicos Patriarch,
of the East.

London,
February 1937.

PREFACE

THE Nestorian churches, which constitute the oldest surviving schism from the Catholic Church of the early centuries, were almost completely isolated from the rest of Christendom for over a millennium. That fact alone makes the study of their history interesting, though at the same time it has greatly reduced their significance in the general trend of ecclesiastical history. Consequently, little attention is usually given to them. In so far as the study of theology is concerned not much is lost, nor have they had much influence in the moulding of civilizations, Christian or otherwise. But their history is of value in showing how Christianity was able to survive centuries of subjection, for during the greater part of their history the Nestorian Christians constituted a despised minority in the midst of populations owning allegiance to other faiths.

In the following chapters an attempt will be made to give a concise account of their fortunes. At the outset, however, it must be stated that the degree of accuracy to be expected in such a history is not comparable with that which can be looked for in histories dealing with events in Europe. For this there are several reasons. First, the sources are fewer, and it is not so often possible to check one source against another. It is therefore sometimes impossible to check a source of information except by internal evidence, and when some of the matter is obviously legendary, the nature of the real facts is often entirely a matter of opinion.

Secondly, there is not the same sure framework of secular history. Much of the work of the Nestorians was done among peoples whose records are scanty and unreliable, and even when the secular history, as in Persia, is fairly complete and trustworthy, it is not always possible to relate the fortunes of the churches to the general events of the time. This is due to the fact that their influence on general affairs was usually so much less than has been the case in Europe, so that cross references between secular and ecclesiastical history are not so frequent.

Thirdly, the sources are difficult of access and difficult to use. A history of the Nestorian churches, compiled entirely from original sources, would necessitate a knowledge of at least a dozen Oriental languages and leisure to travel over a great part of Europe and Asia. It is inevitable, therefore, that much must be accepted at second hand, and the best that can be done is to compile a continuous history from such material as is accessible. Such a work can naturally make little claim to originality except in the exercise of critical judgement in selecting and arranging the material; hence indebtedness to former writers is to be taken as implicit throughout the book. To avoid undue multiplication of footnotes, it is to be understood that mention of a book in the bibliography implies that use has been made of it, and as a rule references will only

be given in footnotes when it is probable that the
actual authority for a particular statement may be
desired, when sentences are quoted almost verbatim,
or when it is intended to indicate that the fact or
opinion quoted is not necessarily accepted by the
present writer.

As to the accuracy of facts, only what seems reasonably probable will be recorded. It must be understood,
however, that there is often considerable difference of
opinion as to what should be accepted and what
rejected; such expressions as 'it seems probable,' 'it is
possible,' and the like, will therefore be sometimes
employed to indicate a degree of uncertainty. As to
dates, many of them are only approximate, even when
circa is not prefixed. In the case of the lists of the
patriarchs the main differences of opinion will be
indicated.

The spelling of proper names and titles presents
another problem. When an Anglicized form exists
which is generally familiar as the name of a person or
persons in ancient history, that form will be used. Thus
it seems undesirable to replace names like John,
Timothy, Theodore, and Cyril by more correct but
less familiar forms. On the other hand, some Anglicized forms look out of place in ancient settings, and
Georgius is therefore preferred to George. Forms such
as Nestor, Diodore, and Dioscor will also be rejected
in favour of Nestorius, Diodorus, and Dioscorus,
because in such cases the Anglicized form has no
currency except with reference to those persons.

Latin and Greek names give little trouble, except

that it is occasionally doubtful whether to use the Latin or the Greek form. For example, *Catholicus* or *Katholikos* serves equally well, though in general Latinized forms will be preferred. Mixed forms are usually to be avoided, though the present patriarch has adopted the form *Catholicos*, as may be seen in the Foreword. But Oriental names present greater difficulty, as so many systems of transliteration have been used, and the same name may occur in upwards of a dozen different guises. Fortescue discusses the matter at some length in the preface to his *Lesser Eastern Churches*,[1] and ends by adding yet another system. The methods recommended by the British Association are in several instances already out-moded. It has therefore been considered best to follow in the main the usage of the latest edition (the fourteenth) of the *Encyclopædia Britannica*, though, as might be expected, it is not always consistent from article to article, nor invariably to be endorsed. But as it is the most generally recognized authority, it seems best to follow it.

This involves adopting some forms which are not yet popular, mostly in a small group of Arabic words. As Arabic only uses the three vowels *a*, *i* and *u*, no other vowels should be used in transliterating pure Arabic words. Unfortunately, in the past *e* has often been put instead of *a* or *i*, and *o* instead of *u*. Thus familiar words like *Moslem* and *Omar* should, without doubt, correctly be rendered *Muslim* and *Umar*. The same applies to *Abu Bekr*, *Othman*, and *Omayyad*, which should be *Abu Bakr*, *Uthman*, and *Umayyad*.

[1] pp. vi–viii.

There is not the same compunction in adopting the spelling *Muhammad* for the Arabian prophet. The much-used *Mahomet* is an error which has no defence but age. Even so long ago as the end of the eighteenth century Assemani called attention to it: 'Per id tempus innotuit Mohammed, quem vulgo Mahometum dicimus, Tajorum seu Arabum propheta.'[1] An additional objection to *Mahomet* is that it gives no derivatives. Although the faith and followers of Muhammad should be termed *Islam* and *Muslims* respectively, it sometimes happens that connexion with the prophet himself needs to be emphasized. In such cases, and only in such cases, *Muhammadanism* and *Muhammadans* may be used. Other forms such as *Mahommed*, *Mohammed*, and their derivatives, are also better discarded. They have forfeited consideration by their very variety. But the *Encyclopædia Britannica* is conservative with regard to *Koran*, not adopting *Quran*.

Usually only one form of spelling will be put in the text, except that, in direct quotations, if the form of a name differs more than slightly from that in general use, the usual form will be added in brackets or as a footnote. But as some names have variants so different that it might not be easy to recognize them as the same person or place, a supplemental index has been added listing some of the more usual alternatives (pp. 223–227). This supplemental index is by no means exhaustive, but it may help readers to trace names they may have met elsewhere in forms different from those given in this work, and by analogy may serve to indicate

[1] *Bibliotheca Orientalis*, III. ii. 94.

the general nature of such variations, so that names not listed will often be safely identified.   Thus it will be seen that *a* and *e*, *i* and *e*, *u* and *o*, *k* and *c*, *q* and *k*, *k* and *ch*, *w* and *v*, are often interchanged; that *h* may be inserted or omitted at the beginning or end of a word, or inserted or omitted after *g*, *s*, *t*, and other letters; that the Arabic article *al* is sometimes retained and sometimes dropped, and when retained is sometimes hyphened and sometimes joined directly to its noun.   But diacritical marks of every kind, accents, quantities, and breathings, have been omitted throughout, except in quotations from Greek, so that a form such as *Ḳalā'ūn* would be listed simply as *Kalaun*.   Nor are variants listed which depend merely on the presence or absence of a hyphen, such as *Il-Khan* and *Ilkhan*, or writing a name divided or run together, such as *Bar Sauma* and *Barsauma*.   It must also be realized that some of the forms given in the supplemental index are quite indefensible: they are not approved, they are merely listed for reference.

Not only will the supplemental index be of use for tracing variants in the spelling of the same name, but it will enable the various changes in the name of the same town to be followed, a frequent cause of confusion. Many towns have had their names changed by conquerors, or have had their names changed for other reasons, or have had different names in different languages.   Thus Seleucia, named after Seleucus Nicator in the third century B.C., was renamed Veh-Ardashir (Beth Ardashir) by Ardashir (Artaxerxes) I in the third century A.D., though the old name remained in use side by side with the new one. A third name for the same place was provided by the Arabs in the seventh century, who named it, jointly with Ctesiphon, al-Madaïn. Thus many towns must be recognized under two or even three quite different names, as well as under varying forms of the same name. Usually the same form will be used throughout for the same town, rather than different forms appropriate to the various periods. Thus Jundishapur is an Arabic form. In the Persian period Gondisapor might be preferable, or Beth Lapat, the Syriac name of the same place. But to avoid confusion Jundishapur will generally be used, and will be added in brackets even when another form has to be employed.

The connotations of a few words need to be defined: *Roman Empire* will be used throughout for what is usually styled the Eastern Roman or Byzantine Empire, whose capital was Constantinople (Byzantium); for the justification of this usage see the *Cambridge Medieval History*, Vol. IV., pp. vii–viii. The words *schism* and *heresy* will be used to mean the separation, administratively and doctrinally respectively, of a person or group from a church to which they formerly belonged, and must be taken as simply descriptive of historic fact, without in any way implying whether the action or opinion was right or wrong. In the same way people will be accorded without qualification the names and descriptions they claimed for themselves, whether Patriarch, Bishop, Priest, Church, or Christian. Thus the word Church will be used where some might prefer sect; but the use of the word is not to be taken as involving any judgement. Similarly, when the word sect is used, it is not necessarily derogatory: it simply means a part cut off from a whole or from a greater part.

As to the general arrangement of the material, it is very difficult to set it out satisfactorily. It is hoped that the analytical table of contents on pp. 19–20 will make the general plan sufficiently clear, and that cross-references and the index will suffice as aids in tracing the events connected with a given person or place. Rather more general history has been introduced than some might think necessary; but without it the story moves against a nebulous background, and so loses much of its coherence.

AUBREY R. VINE

Reading,
February 1937.

CONTENTS

ANALYTICAL TABLE OF CONTENTS

Chapter I

THE ORIGIN OF NESTORIANISM

Nestorius, a fifth-century bishop of Constantinople, has provided a name for a heresy which he did not originate, possibly did not even hold, and for a Church which he did not found. Nevertheless, his name has become so firmly associated with a certain Christological theory and with the churches which have held that theory that it is not now easy to find terms equally definite but more exactly descriptive. Nestorianism, therefore, must be understood to mean the Christology supposedly held by Nestorius, though not originated by him, and the Nestorian churches the churches holding to the Nestorian Christology. It should perhaps be remarked that these churches have never officially used the title Nestorian to describe themselves, though they have not usually objected to it; their own designation is 'Church of the East.' But by retaining the term 'Nestorian churches' emphasis is laid on the fact that their characteristic is theological rather than merely geographical.

The formation of these churches into a separate communion was a gradual process, which may be deemed to have reached completion when Babai, Patriarch of Seleucia-Ctesiphon (487–502), declared that the churches of Persia and other churches which acknowledged him as their spiritual head were henceforward to be completely independent of the churches in the Roman Empire, and that Nestorian theology was to be the basis of their doctrine. It is hardly desirable, however, to begin their history at that point. It is necessary to understand what Nestorianism was, why it was condemned by the orthodoxy of the Roman Empire, how it came to be associated with the churches in Persia, and how those churches came to separate themselves from the rest of Christendom. This will necessitate a brief survey of the course of Christology during the latter part of the fourth century and the earlier part of the fifth.

The Council of Nicæa[1] (325) had established orthodox doctrine as to the full deity of Christ; and though the repercussions of the Arian controversy[2] continued for some years, the Council of Constantinople (381) reaffirmed the creed of Nicæa, and from that time the Nicene Creed was accepted without question

[1] The first Œcumenical Council. Eight Church Councils are reckoned as œcumenical (general, universal): Nicæa, 325; Constantinople, 381; Ephesus, 431; Chalcedon, 451; Constantinople, 553; Constantinople, 680; Nicæa, 787; Constantinople, 869. The Greeks, however, do not admit the last one in this list; if they reckon an eighth, it is that of Constantinople in 879.

[2] Arius taught that Christ was created 'out of things which are not' (ἐξ οὐκ ὄντων); and although prior to and superior to all the rest of creation, was not of the same essence (οὐσία) as God the Father. The Council of Nicæa was called by the Emperor Constantine to resolve the acute controversy thus aroused. This Council drew up the Nicene Creed, which declares that Christ is the only begotten Son of God, begotten (not created) from the essence of the Father, and of like essence (ὁμοούσιος) to Him. It also places the generation of Christ outside time. (τοὺς δὲ λέγοντας ἦν ποτε ὅτε οὐκ ἦν . . . τούτους ἀναθεματίζει ἡ καθολικὴ καὶ ἀποστολικὴ ἐκκλησία.)

by orthodoxy within the Roman Empire. Indeed, soon afterwards, in 383, the Emperor Theodosius I declared Arianism to be contrary to Roman law, and the Nicene Creed thus became the official creed of both Church and Empire.

But the Nicene emphasis on the deity of Christ brought into fresh prominence the problem of His humanity: if Christ were fully deity, to what extent and in what way could He also be human? This problem, which had exercised the Gnostics[1] in the second century and Origen[2] in the third, was brought into prominence again by Apollinarius. Apollinarius, bishop of Laodicæa (*ob.* 390), had put forward a Christology based on the Greek idea of man as tripartite: body, animal soul, and intellect (σῶμα, ψυχή, νοῦς). In Christ, intellect was replaced by the Logos (λόγος), the eternally generated Word of God, which Apollinarius held to be fully deity. This view had been condemned at the Council of Constantinople on the ground that without a human intellect Christ could not be regarded as really man. Moreover, if Christ were not completely human, His sacrifice as man for men would be to that extent defective; as Gregory of Nazianzus cogently put it, 'that which is unassumed is unhealed' (τὸ γὰρ ἀπρόσληπτον ἀθεράπευτον). But the problem was not solved by the mere rejecting of an unsatisfactory solution: it was

[1] The Gnostics regarded Christ as a divine being, but not as deity; and they taught that His human form was a mere appearance (δόκησις). This view of Christ's nature is known as *docetism*.

[2] Origen taught that Christ was the fusion of the continuously generated Son of God with an untainted human soul, this fusion dwelling in a human body.

only brought into greater prominence. Two modes of approach to the problem now became clearly differentiated, which were adopted by the school of Alexandria and the school of Antioch respectively.

The Alexandrian school, at one time noted for its comprehensive scholarship, had gradually adopted a more conservative attitude, and had become the stronghold of orthodox doctrine. Its influence was paramount in Egypt, and of great consequence throughout the West. During the earlier part of the fifth century the Alexandrian school had a remarkably capable representative in Cyril (376–444), who had been bishop of Alexandria since 412. His teaching may be summarized thus: the Logos, pre-existing as a hypostatic distinction in the Godhead, united with Himself complete manhood. But the union was not in the nature of a mere contact or bond: the Logos had not only assumed flesh, but had become flesh. So Christ was the Logos united with a complete human being; but so perfect was the union that the two natures, divine and human, constituted only one person. (This union of the two natures into one person is referred to as the hypostatic union.) Nevertheless, the two natures were not confused or mingled: 'the flesh is flesh and not deity, even if it has become flesh of God'; so that the one person still possessed the two complete natures, and could assess experiences according to each of them: as the Logos, His divine nature was impassible and unchangeable; but through the humanity He had taken to Himself, He entered into all human feelings. Thus one person experienced through two perfectly united natures. This ability to experience through both natures, although there is only one person, is explained as due to an interchange (ἀντίδοσις) between the natures of their respective characteristics, the 'communicatio idiomatum' of Latin theology. This last phrase is difficult to render precisely, but perhaps 'sharing of characteristics' may serve. In this way the experiences of the God-man are both truly divine and truly human. (It will be seen that all this involves one rather serious difficulty: the Incarnation is simply an event in the eternal life of the Logos, but a beginning for the human life of His assumed manhood; but though there are two natures, there is only one person; one of the natures must therefore be impersonal. As it is obvious that the Logos cannot be regarded as impersonal, the human nature must be so regarded. Harnack considers that this reduces Cyril's position to monophysitism, but Loofs maintains that it does not necessarily do so, so long as the human nature is maintained to be complete and real.) To make the union of natures absolute and complete, it seemed necessary to postulate that the process of fusion proceeded *in utero* from the moment of conception. It would follow that the Virgin Mary, in bearing the man Jesus, bore also the Logos, that is, Deity: the Virgin 'had borne the Incarnate Word according to the flesh.' Now while this is quite logical and unexceptionable, the same idea, when expressed by applying the title Theotokos (θεοτόκος, 'bearer of God') to the Virgin Mary, was in danger of extension beyond its proper limits. Rightly understood, the epithet is innocuous. But if loosely interpreted as 'Mother of God,' there would obviously be danger of the Virgin Mary being popularly regarded almost as a goddess. Subsequent events were to prove what a storm centre this word could provide. The Alexandrian school, therefore, postulated the full deity and the full humanity of Christ, and the perfect union of the two complete natures in one person.

But the Antiochene school, which dominated Syria and Asia Minor, approached the problem from quite a different standpoint. Their approach was based not so much on theological reasoning as on the interpretation of objective historical data, and to them the primary reality was the historic Jesus. Indeed, the school of Antioch is often referred to as the Syrian historico-exegetical school. Two particularly able teachers had given form to the Antiochene Christology, Diodorus of Tarsus, founder of the school, and Theodore of Mopsuestia (*ob.* 429), his most famous pupil. Of Diodorus not a great deal is known, as all but a few fragments of his works have been lost. But the teaching of Theodore can with fair certainty be reconstructed, and it was undoubtedly he who gave definite form to the views for which Nestorius was later condemned. Theodore taught that Christ was primarily and fully man, but that from before His birth God's special complacency (εὐδοκία) dwelt in Him. Theodore identifies this complacency with the Logos, carefully distinguishing the Logos from the Being of God, which is omnipresent and therefore indwells all men and things indifferently. In addition to the

Logos, at His baptism Christ received the Holy Ghost, by whose power His subsequent work was done. Theodore regarded the union of manhood, Logos and Holy Ghost as progressive and not completely perfected until the Ascension. Even so, the union was regarded as due to a perfect complacency between divinity and humanity rather than to a union of essence: it is 'according to complacency, not according to essence' (κατ' εὐδοκίαν, οὐ κατ' οὐσίαν). Consequently the divine and human natures are in conjunction as though joined by some kind of bond (συνάφεια), rather than in a state of true unification (ἕνωσις), though it must be admitted that Theodore does occasionally use the latter word. Theodore thus emphasizes the full humanity of Christ, but gives no satisfactory account of the way in which the divine and human natures constitute one person. Indeed, although Theodore asserted the full and unique Sonship of Christ, his Christology leaves the impression of a person specially favoured, guided and empowered by God, but hardly one to whom the term Deity could be applied.

Among those who were trained under the influence of Theodore and his teaching was Nestorius. Of his origin and early life little is known, except that he was born at Germanicia near Mount Taurus in Syria. After a period as a monk at the monastery of Euprepius near Antioch, he became a presbyter at Antioch, where he gained some distinction both as a preacher and for the austerity of his personal life. But he did not come into special prominence until difficulty arose in finding a suitable successor to Sisinnius as bishop of Constantinople. Sisinnius had died in December 427, and conflicting local interests had rendered the appointment of a Constantinopolitan unwise. Looking to Antioch, Nestorius seemed suitable, so in April 428 he was appointed to the vacant see.

At first the appointment appears to have been acceptable to all sections at Constantinople, both clerical and lay; and although the choice had been made by the Court, the monkish party, whose leader was the Archimandrite Dalmatius, was apparently quite satisfied. Unfortunately, the satisfaction was of short duration. Nestorius became involved in a controversy as to the propriety of applying the term Theotokos to the Virgin Mary. Whether Nestorius himself precipitated the dispute by attacking the term in a sermon he preached early in 429, whether he was drawn into it by supporting his presbyter, Anastasius, who had attacked the term, or whether he merely became involved in a dispute that was already raging when he arrived at Constantinople, cannot perhaps be certainly decided.[1] But the matter did arise, and Nestorius became unhappily implicated. It would appear that he was personally quite opposed to the term, and suggested replacing it by Christotokos (χριστοτόκος, 'bearer of Christ'), saying, 'Mary did not bear the Godhead; she bore a man who was the organ of the Godhead.' But this compromise was not of much help in easing matters, and he eventually yielded so far as to allow the use of the title Theotokos,

[1] For a discussion on this point, see Loofs, *Nestorius*, pp. 28–32.

provided that its popular implications were not unduly pressed.

Had the controversy been purely local, it might have died down and done no lasting harm. But Cyril, bishop of Alexandria, took it upon himself to interfere. His motives have been much discussed. It may be that he was genuinely convinced that the term Theotokos had to be defended if the full deity of Christ were to be maintained. The word had been used by Athanasius and possibly by Origen, and was regarded as a defence against unitarian tendencies. But less disinterested motives were certainly present. He was jealous for the power of his see and of himself, and was anxious that Constantinople should be influenced by Alexandria rather than by Antioch. He probably also saw the dispute as a challenge from Antiochene Christology to Alexandrian Christology, and he may have thought that successful interference would establish the ascendancy of the see of Alexandria over both Antioch and Constantinople, thus helping to maintain Alexandria against the rapidly increasing prestige of Rome. Nestorius suggested an even less creditable motive: that Cyril entered into the dispute in order to divert attention from accusations against himself; and there is certainly some evidence pointing that way.[1]

But whatever the motives may have been, Cyril did interfere. He prepared his way with care, fostering enmity against Nestorius by agents in Constantinople, and taking steps to gain Celestine, bishop of Rome, on to his own side. Rome was probably to some extent

[1] See Loofs, op. cit., pp. 33–41.

inclined to side with Cyril rather than with Nestorius owing to the fact that Nestorius had received at Constantinople some Pelagians who had been banished from Rome. Eventually Cyril was able to persuade the Pope to condemn Nestorius, which was done at a synod at Rome on August 11th, 430. A letter was drawn up notifying Nestorius that unless he recanted within ten days he would be regarded as excommunicated. This letter was entrusted to Cyril to deliver. But before forwarding it, Cyril held a synod at Alexandria, and condemned Nestorius in similar terms to those used at Rome, adding twelve anathemas[1] which Nestorius was to accept within ten days or be excommunicated. The very first of these anathemas shows the way in which the rejection of the term Theotokos was assumed by Cyril to imply a questioning of the deity of Christ, and so to be contrary to the creed of Nicæa: 'If any one does not confess Emmanuel to be truly God, and the Holy Virgin therefore the bearer of God [Theotokos], for she bore according to the flesh flesh which had become the Word [Logos] of God: let him be accursed.'

Meanwhile Nestorius had not been inactive. He saw the way events were tending, and knew that nothing but his downfall would satisfy Cyril. He thereupon took a step which he hoped would save himself: to void the excommunications sent from Rome and Alexandria he besought the Emperor Theodosius II, who was still favourable to him, to call an œcumenical council to investigate the whole matter.

[1] They are quoted in full by Gieseler, *Ecclesiastical History*, i. 397–398.

The emperor agreed to do so, and issued an order accordingly, which was dated November 19th, 430, thus preceding by a narrow but sufficient margin the delivery to Nestorius of the communications from Rome and Alexandria, which were received on December 6th, 430.

The œcumenical council was called for Whit-Sunday, June 7th, 431, and was to meet at Ephesus. The proceedings reflected unfavourably on all concerned. The Syrian bishops, under the leadership of John of Antioch, arrived more than a fortnight late, and the Roman legates still later. Cyril, meanwhile, had insisted on the council being opened. The emperor's commissioner, Count Candidian, protested in vain, and the proceedings began. Nestorius refused to appear before so unrepresentative an assembly, consisting for the most part of Egyptian partisans of Cyril. He was therefore condemned *in absentia*, a condemnation received in Ephesus with tumultuous approval, Memnon, the bishop of Ephesus, being favourable to Cyril. When the Syrians arrived, however, they at once joined with Nestorius in holding a rival council, at which they in turn deposed Cyril and Memnon. But when the Roman legates arrived, they sided with Cyril.

Theodosius, acquainted with this unseemly impasse, appointed a second commissioner, Count John, who cut the Gordian knot by confirming all three depositions, that of Nestorius by the Alexandrian section of the council, and those of Cyril and Memnon by the Syrian section. Nestorius was sent back to the monastery of Euprepius, which just over three years earlier had witnessed his glorious departure for Constantinople. There he remained, no longer a figure of consequence, for the next four years. Cyril and Memnon fared better, probably owing to Cyril's skill in gaining friends at Court and elsewhere by intrigue and bribery. Cyril soon escaped from custody and returned to Alexandria, where he resumed his episcopate as though no deposition had been pronounced. He had evidently been able to gain the favour of the emperor, and of the emperor's elder sister Pulcheria, whose influence was considerable. A little later Memnon was allowed to resume his office at Ephesus.

As to the doctrinal problems, nothing had really been settled at the Council of Ephesus, or rather at the two party councils. Theodosius, therefore, summoned each group to send delegates to a further conference at Chalcedon; but when it became clear that no decision was likely to be reached, Theodosius officially dissolved it, merely expressing general approval of the orthodox position. Although it formulated no creed and settled no problem, the Council of Ephesus has to be reckoned the third Œcumenical Council.

The events of the next few years reflect the astuteness of Cyril and the weakness of the Antiochians. The successor of Nestorius as bishop of Constantinople was Maximian, of whom Cyril approved. Having now the friendship of the emperor and the co-operation of the new bishop of Constantinople, Cyril proceeded by intrigue and bribery to force the Antiochians to come to an understanding with him; for they continued to

hold Nestorius in esteem and regarded Cyril's twelve
anathemas as heretical. But Cyril's methods eventually triumphed, and in 433 Alexandrians and Antiochians made their peace. The terms were that the
Antiochians should acknowledge the validity of Cyril's
section of the council, at any rate as regards the anathematizing of Nestorius, though Cyril's twelve anathemas
were not specifically endorsed; and that the Alexandrians should accept an Antiochian confession of
faith. This agreement healed the breach between
Alexandria and Antioch. In effect, the Syrians had
sacrificed Nestorius in order to secure peace with
Egypt and the West; and John, bishop of Antioch, who
had been foremost among the Syrian negotiators, now
found Nestorius, his former friend, a grave embarrass-
ment. There were, therefore, few to voice protest or
regret when in 435 Nestorius was banished, first to
Petra in Arabia, and then to Oasis in Egypt, and
Theodosius issued an edict ordering all his writings to
be destroyed and his adherents to be called Simonians.

Though the influence of Nestorius was thus completely ended in the school of Antioch, which had
formerly regarded him with pride, and although he
was now disowned by the great majority of his original
supporters, the Syrian bishops, the position which he
had represented was by no means altogether forsaken.
Many of the teachers in the important theological
school at Edessa were still attached to the doctrinal
system of Theodore of Mopsuestia, and approved
neither of the events which had taken place at the
Council of Ephesus nor of the discreditable way in
Cc

which peace had been arranged between Cyril and John. Thus it came about that the next scenes in the fortunes of Nestorianism were set at Edessa.

But before passing on to Edessa, it may be desirable to complete the personal history of Nestorius himself. There is not much to relate. Soon after his banishment to Oasis he was captured by Blemmyes, marauding nomads. They released him, evidently near Panopolis, for from there he wrote a letter to the governor, lest he should be suspected of seeking to flee. The governor decided to send him to Elephantine, but changed his mind and sent him back to Panopolis. His place of exile seems to have been changed several times, and these removals and his broken health must have made his life very hard. He must have survived, however, for about fifteen years after his banishment, as his *Bazaar of Heraclides* shows that he had heard of the death of Theodosius (450). The only relief to his exile was the conviction that Leo and Flavian were inclining to his position: 'It is my doctrine,' he wrote, 'which Leo and Flavian are upholding!' He probably died before the Council of Chalcedon in 451, and was thus saved the humiliation of knowing that it, too, had condemned him. As to personal ambition, he had abandoned it altogether, and never sought recall from exile. Perhaps he feared that his return would only precipitate further trouble, and he preferred to remain as he was rather than to do that: 'The goal of my earnest wish, then,' he wrote, 'is that God may be blessed on earth as in heaven. But as for Nestorius, let him be anathema! Only let them say of God what

I pray that they should say. I am prepared to endure and to suffer all for Him. And would that all men by anathematizing me might attain to a reconciliation with God.'

Thus died Nestorius, at a place unknown, at a date unfixed, whose brief episcopate at Constantinople precipitated events which placed his name for ever on the pages of history. A just estimate of him is not easily made. Although his fate arouses our sympathy, his conduct during his first months at Constantinople suggests that he would have been equally hard on worsted opponents of his own. In one of his first sermons before the emperor he said: 'Purge me, O Cæsar, the earth of heretics, and I in return will give thee heaven. Stand by me in putting down the heretics, and I will stand by thee in putting down the Persians.' He soon tried to implement these words by beginning a vigorous campaign of suppression against Arians, Novatians, and Quartodecimans; so that if Nestorius had gained the upper hand, it may be questioned whether he would have treated Cyril any better than Cyril treated him.

It was unfortunate that the purely theological dispute was so complicated by other considerations. Theologically, there is no doubt whatever that Cyril was far more capable than Nestorius. Cyril recognized what were the essentials of a sound Christology and boldly stated them, not shrinking from any implications. Nestorius had not so keen a mind, and possibly never clearly distinguished between Godhead and deity nor grasped the idea which 'communicatio idiomatum' was meant to convey. His main concern was to prevent misuse of the term Theotokos, but that issue soon involved him in problems which were too deep for him.

It may, however, be safely asserted that Nestorius never held the crude view of Christ's person which is implied by the formula 'Two natures, two persons, and one presence.'[1] If he was a heretic, as Bedjan[2] and Nau[3] maintain, it was his misfortune and not his choice. Loofs[4] and Bethune-Baker[5] take a more complacent view; but sympathy with a tragic fate must not lead us to condone defective theology. Yet there is no escaping the conclusion that Nestorius was unfortunate in having an opponent, not simply so capable, but also so astute, so determined, and in some ways apparently so unscrupulous, as Cyril. Even if Cyril was theologically right, his methods were not always commendable, and it would have been more satisfactory if sound Christology could have been upheld with less acrimony and more charity.

[1] See p. 54.
[2] German editor of the *Bazaar of Heraclides*.
[3] Translator into French of the *Bazaar of Heraclides*.
[4] *Nestoriana* and *Nestorius*.
[5] *Nestorius and his Teaching*.

CHAPTER II

TRANSITION TO PERSIA

ALTHOUGH Nestorius was banished, the ideas which he had represented were not left without exponents. As has already been indicated, there was a strong element favourable to Nestorian views at the theological school at Edessa. The attitude of this school is of particular significance because at it most of the clergy for the churches in Persia received their training. They were trained at Edessa in Roman territory rather than in Persia, owing to the frequency and severity of the Persian persecutions at this period. (See the list on pp. 81–82.) At the time of the Nestorian controversy Rabbulas had been bishop of Edessa since 412, and Ibas was a presbyter of the church and head of the theological school. Rabbulas seems to have vacillated in his opinion of Nestorius; or perhaps he was swayed by considerations of policy rather than of doctrine. He had at first been unfavourable to Nestorius, preaching a sermon directed against him at Constantinople. At the Council of Ephesus, however, he had supported Nestorius against Cyril. But when John of Antioch had come to terms with Cyril, Rabbulas was among those who forsook Nestorius for the sake of peace with Alexandria and the West. From that time (433) till his death in 435 he did what he could to maintain harmonious relations with the other churches of the Roman Empire.

But Ibas had remained true to the Nestorian position. He was a devoted disciple of Theodore of Mopsuestia, whose works he had translated into Syriac; and thinking that Nestorius represented the views of Theodore, Ibas had sided with him at the Council of Ephesus. Subsequently he became less favourable to Nestorius personally, as is evidenced by his letter to Maris.[1] But he never departed from the doctrinal positions of Theodore, and as that is what is really meant by Nestorianism, Ibas must be reckoned a consistent Nestorian.

Not only in the theological school, but also among the laity in Edessa, there were very many who followed Ibas rather than Rabbulas. It was, therefore, not surprising that when Rabbulas died in 435 Ibas was chosen as bishop of Edessa, which see he occupied from 436 to 457. He had not held his episcopate many years when the controversy concerning the two natures of Christ broke out again. As at the time when Cyril and Nestorius were the protagonists, it was not only theological interests that were involved. Cyril had died in 444, and had been succeeded in his bishopric

[1] This letter was written to 'Maris, bishop of Beth Ardashir' (i.e. Seleucia). But as the bishop of Seleucia-Ctesiphon at this time was Dadyeshu (421–456), Labourt suggests that Maris is really simply the Syriac *Mari*, 'My Lord,' and not a proper name. The letter denounces Rabbulas, and is Nestorian in tone, though Ibas seems to have lost regard for Nestorius himself. It was one of the 'Three Chapters' condemned at the Council of Constantinople in 553, the fifth Œcumenical Council. (*Mar*, *Mari*, and *Mart* represent the Syriac for *Lord*, *My Lord*, and *Lady* respectively.)

by Dioscorus, his archdeacon. The new bishop was as jealous for the prestige of his see as his predecessor had been, and was equally anxious to assert his authority over the East, particularly over Constantinople. There were three men whose downfall he was consequently eager to compass. One was Flavian, bishop of Constantinople; he was anxious to humble him so that the authority of Alexandria over Constantinople might again be asserted, just as it had been by Theophilus over Chrysostom and by Cyril over Nestorius. The other two he held in enmity were the two leading representatives of the condemned Nestorian Christology: Ibas of Edessa, and Theodoret of Cyrus.

The first real opportunity for Dioscorus came in 448, when Flavian deposed Eutyches, archimandrite of a monastery near Constantinople, for denying the reality of the two natures in Christ. He appears to have taught that there was a 'blending and confusion' (σύγκρασις καὶ σύγχυσις) of Godhead and manhood at the Incarnation. The deposition took place at a synod held at Constantinople. But Dioscorus refused to acknowledge the legality of the synod, and showed his disapprobation by entering into communion with Eutyches. The Emperor Theodosius II thereupon ordered a general council to be called at Ephesus to inquire into the matter. Both sides meanwhile appealed to Leo, bishop of Rome. Leo delivered his judgement in a document usually referred to as the Tome of Leo, in which he reiterated the position already established in the West, that Christ had two natures in one person; and condemned the opinion of Eutyches, which he took to imply that before the Incarnation there were two natures, but that when the divine and human blended only one nature resulted, the divine. This statement of the view, whether or not it is exactly what Eutyches taught, it called monophysitism. Leo thus maintained that the question had already been settled, so that no council was needed.

Nevertheless, the council was held. It met at Ephesus in 449, and Dioscorus presided. More by intimidation than argument, Dioscorus had everything his own way: Eutyches was acquitted and reinstated, Flavian and his supporters were deposed, and Ibas and Theodoret were deprived of their sees and excommunicated. The whole of the proceedings was undignified and violent, so much so that Flavian died as the result of the rough treatment he received there. Leo, indignant at the slight implied upon himself, declared that the council was nothing better than a gathering of robbers (lactrocinium), and of no authority. Leo's epithet was apt enough to be adopted, and the assembly is usually referred to as the Robber Council or Latrocinium. It is not reckoned among the Œcumenical Councils.

Thus Dioscorus triumphed, and Alexandria held a sway over the East as absolute as that of Rome over the West. But the triumph was shortlived. The next year, 450, Theodosius II died, and imperial support for Dioscorus ceased. Pulcheria, sister of Theodosius, became empress, and strengthened her position by marrying Marcian, who was able and respected both as a senator and a general. One of their first acts was to call a council to reconsider the verdicts which had been reached so precipitately at Ephesus two years before. A council was accordingly held at Chalcedon in 451. The Tome of Leo was endorsed, and Dioscorus was condemned and deposed. Shortly afterwards he was banished to Gangra in Paphlagonia, where he died in 454. The cases of Ibas and Theodoret presented greater difficulty. To complete the discomfiture of Dioscorus it seemed desirable to reinstate them, though as the leading Nestorians remaining within the empire, simple reinstatement was hardly practicable. After much heated discussion it was agreed to reinstate them on condition that they anathematized both Nestorius and Eutyches, and accepted the Tome of Leo. This they did, though with what feelings and mental reservations it would be interesting to know. Probably they regarded themselves as followers of Theodore rather than of Nestorius, and accepted the only possible way of escape from their unfortunate situation. But it was common knowledge that they had not really changed their views.

Thus Ibas was able to resume his see in 451. But the state of affairs at Edessa had greatly changed since he was acclaimed bishop in 436. There was now quite a considerable section against him, led by four of his own presbyters. They had caused trouble for him even before the Robber Council of Ephesus, by making various trivial charges against him. Synods at Antioch and Tyre had failed to substantiate these charges, but they had naturally lowered his prestige. The Nestorian party at Edessa was steadily declining, and after the death of Ibas in 457, it became increasingly difficult for Edessa to remain a centre of Nestorianism in an empire where Nestorianism was condemned. Losing hold on church and city, it lingered on in the theological school until 489, when the school was closed and destroyed by order of the Emperor Zeno, the Nestorian remnant fleeing into Persia. That was the end of Nestorianism in the Roman Empire, its final condemnation being delivered by the Council of Constantinople, the fifth Œcumenical Council, in 553, which condemned the person and writings of Theodore of Mopsuestia, the real author of Nestorianism.

But while Nestorianism was declining in the Roman Empire, it was in the ascendant in Persia. The majority of the Persian clergy had for many years been trained at Edessa, so that Nestorian views were naturally prevalent among them. There was also in Persia an ardent advocate of Nestorianism in the person of Barsumas. Barsumas had been a disciple and friend of Ibas in the days when Rabbulas was bishop of Edessa and Ibas head of the theological school. Rabbulas had expelled him on account of his pronounced Nestorianism, and he had gone to Nisibis, just over the border into Persian territory. There he was well received, became first bishop of Nisibis in 457, and founded a theological school.

As a theological opinion Nestorianism had therefore been long in evidence in Persia. But after the Council of Chalcedon it assumed a new significance. The Persian Government had opposed Christianity partly because it was the religion of their national rivals, the

Romans. But now that Nestorianism had been condemned and Nestorians were seeking refuge in Persia,
there was no longer any danger that such a form of
Christianity would be a link with an alien power; on
the contrary, it would be politically wise to encourage
Nestorianism among Persian Christians, so as to
alienate them from Christians in the Roman Empire.
This was accordingly done, and King Peroz (457–484)
gave up persecuting the Christians, except for a persecution in 465.   But as this was directed against those
who wished to remain in communion with the Church
of the Roman Empire, it acted more as a stimulus to
Nestorianism than as a deterrent from Christianity.
Indeed, it is said that Barsumas himself took an active
part in this persecution, telling Peroz that it would be
best for the Persian authorities if all Persian Christians
were made to accept Nestorianism. Consequently
three factors were working in the same direction: the
attitude of the Persian Government, the dominant
personality of Barsumas, and the influx of Nestorians
from Edessa. It is therefore not surprising that
Nestorianism and the Christian Church in Persia soon
became practically synonymous.

Nevertheless, it was some time before the Persian
Church became formally Nestorian.   This was because
so much depended upon the attitude of the Persian
Patriarch, the bishop of Seleucia-Ctesiphon. This
position was held by Babowai (457–484), who does not
appear to have favoured Nestorianism. His opposition was probably due to jealousy of Barsumas and a
desire to retain friendly relations with the Church in the

Roman Empire, rather than to theological convictions.
But before considering the conflict of Babowai and
Barsumas, it is desirable to see how the bishop of Seleucia-
Ctesiphon had come to count for so much in Persia.

The Persian churches, separated from the greater
part of Christendom both by national frontiers and
by language, had almost inevitably come to regard
themselves as a unity, and had begun to look for
leadership within their own country rather than in
far away Antioch, in which Patriarchate they were
reckoned. Other things being equal, leadership would
naturally be assumed by the bishop of the most important see. Now Ctesiphon was at this time the
principal place of residence of the Persian kings, and
on the opposite (right) bank of the Tigris stood the still
older city of Seleucia. These two cities[1] constituted
one bishopric, which accounts for the hyphened designation which is always used. Its bishop might
therefore reasonably claim first place in the Persian
episcopate, and as far back as 315, Papa Bar Aggai,
the then bishop of Seleucia-Ctesiphon, had endeavoured at a synod held at Seleucia to assert his primacy
over the other Persian bishops. His claims were only
partially admitted, and the question was not finally
settled until a synod held at Seleucia in 410, at the end
of the episcopate of Isaac, bishop of Seleucia-Ctesiphon
from 399 to 410.[2]

[1] They became increasingly unified, and the Arabs of the seventh
century renamed them with a single name, al-Madaïn. The one
name, however, means 'the (two) cities,' and so to some extent preserves
the fact that they were originally separate entities.

[2] Isaac's date is thus given by Labourt, Kidd, and Fortescue. The
Encyclopædia Britannica, xxi. 722, gives 390–410.

This synod was also notable for another reason, for there the Persian bishops declared their adherence to the decisions reached at the Council of Nicæa in 325, and subscribed to the Nicene Creed. They also laid it down that there should only be one bishop to each see, that ordination of bishops should be by three other bishops, and that Epiphany, Lent, Good Friday and Easter should be observed as elsewhere in the Church. These decisions are noteworthy, as the Nestorian Church of later centuries did not depart from the findings of this synod, which can therefore be taken as the measure of its agreement with catholicity and orthodoxy.

As to the question of primacy, it was decided that the bishop of Seleucia-Ctesiphon should be accounted Primate of the Persian Church, and that in recognition of this pre-eminence he should be given the title Catholicus. The exact meaning of this word is a little obscure. It may have been borrowed from Roman civil usage, where catholicus was a title applied to diocesan[1] ministers of finance; or it may have been adopted to indicate that his authority was 'catholic' (Greek 'throughout the whole') in Persia. But in any case it is quite clear what place they intended the Catholicus to occupy in the Hierarchy: he was to come between the Patriarch and the Metropolitans.

[1] The word 'diocese,' now used almost exclusively as an ecclesiastical term, was originally the name of large divisions in the Roman Empire, such as the diocese of Pontus, the diocese of Thracia, the diocese of Dacia, etc. At the end of the fourth century the Western Roman Empire was divided into six dioceses and the Eastern Roman Empire into seven.

By the fifth century the whole of the Christian Church was regarded as being comprised within four[1] Patriarchates, which had been defined by the Council of Constantinople in 381 as Rome, Constantinople, Alexandria, and Antioch, of which Rome was to be reckoned the first. Christendom was thus divided administratively under four Patriarchs, under whom again were Metropolitans. The Metropolitan was the primate among the bishops in his province, and each bishop was responsible for his own diocese. Thus patriarchates, provinces, and dioceses were respectively controlled by patriarchs, metropolitans,[2] and bishops. It may be pointed out that these all represent degrees of standing among bishops, and not separate orders. Now the Persians wanted the bishopric of Seleucia-Ctesiphon to be ranked higher than the other metropolitans in Persia, and they also wanted all Persian bishops, ordinary bishops and metropolitans alike, to owe their allegiance to the patriarch of Antioch, not directly, but through the bishop of Seleucia-Ctesiphon. Obviously this could only be done by interposing a degree between metropolitan and patriarch, which they accordingly did by making the bishop of Seleucia-Ctesiphon Primate of Persia and Catholicus.

This appointment was the more significant because King Yazdegerd I (399–420) himself approved the organization of the Persian Church on this basis, and issued a firman giving recognition to the Catholicus as

[1] Jerusalem was not made a Patriarchate until a little later, at the Council of Chalcedon, 451.

[2] Later, metropolitans in the West were usually styled archbishops. The terms are practically synonymous.

head of the Persian Christians. They thus became a section of the population with a definite standing, responsible for their own good order, and answerable to the authorities through the Catholicus, who was their accredited link with the civil power. In this way he became in a sense their civil as well as religious head. The only drawback was that in future the Catholicus had to be approved by the King of Persia, which in practice sometimes meant that the office could only be filled by his nominee.

Nevertheless, Yazdegerd was a tolerant monarch to whom the Persian Christians owed a great deal, as he put an end to the Magian[1] idea that Christians were heretics necessarily worthy of death, and gave them an approved status. Such communities within the State, answerable through their own head to the civil authorities, have not been uncommon in the East, and many different terms have been used to describe them, such as rayah (raiyah, raiyyah), dhimmi (dimmi), melet (millah, millet). To describe this condition we shall consistently use the word *melet*, though strictly speaking different terms should be used according to the exact condition and period. Although Yazdegerd put an end to the Magian tendency to persecute Christians on principle, there were quite a number of later persecutions under the Sassanids[2]; but there was always some ostensible excuse for them, and none was so fierce or prolonged as that under Shapur II. Thus from 410

[1] For a note on the Magians, see p. 65.
[2] For a list of the Sassanid Kings, and indications of their attitude toward Christianity, see pp. 81–82.

the Persian Church had a recognized position in the
Persian state, and a Hierarch acknowledged by the
Persian King. From 410, therefore, the Catholicus
is to be reckoned the religious and to some extent the
civil head of the Christians in Persia. These happenings manifestly went far toward developing the idea
of complete religious autonomy. Isaac was considerably helped at this synod, and in the negotiations
with Yazdegerd, by Marutha, bishop of Maiperkat.

The next step was taken at the synod of Markabta in
424, during the catholicate of Dadyeshu (421–456). At
this synod it was declared that the bishop of Seleucia-
Ctesiphon should be the sole head of the Persian
Church, and that no ecclesiastical authority should be
acknowledged as above him. In particular, it was laid
down that 'Easterns shall not complain of their
patriarch to the western patriarchs: every case that
cannot be settled by him shall await the tribunal of
Christ.' This is the first time that the bishop of
Seleucia-Ctesiphon is referred to as patriarch, and,
according to the Roman Catholic point of view,[1] this
declaration placed the Persian Church definitely in a
state of schism. It was not heretical, because no
matters of doctrine were involved as yet. That issue
was to arise later.

But the act of elevating their Catholicus to a Patriarch was of inescapable significance. Until then,[2] no
one had assumed the title unless it had been conferred

---

[1] Fortescue, *Lesser Eastern Churches*, p. 51.
[2] Later, particularly in the West, the title was more loosely used, and
was assumed by many metropolitans without its earlier significance.

upon him by an œcumenical council, so that his elevation
bore the sign of the whole Church's approval. Moreover, the delimitation of the area of a new patriarchate
was a matter for careful adjustment, for it was bound
to involve, to some extent, taking from other patriarchates, as happened when Jerusalem became a
patriarchate. But the Persians boldly took matters
into their own hands and, without consulting any but
themselves, broke off a great area of the patriarchate
of Antioch and constituted it the patriarchate of
Seleucia-Ctesiphon. The patriarch is sometimes also
referred to as Patriarch of the East, or of Babylon.
Curiously enough, Antioch does not seem to have
made any protest. Thus from 424 the Persian Church
was completely separated from the rest of Christendom,
not doctrinally, but administratively. Its supreme
head was the Patriarch of Seleucia-Ctesiphon, who
claimed equality of rank with the other four patriarchs,
but by whom he was in no way recognized.

Such, therefore, was the state of affairs when Barsumas was trying to make the Persian Church definitely
Nestorian. He could not possibly succeed unless he
won over the patriarch, or unless he became patriarch
himself. Practically speaking, Nestorian theology had
dominated Persia for over half a century, but while
Babowai remained patriarch it would not be formally
endorsed.

In 484 Barsumas nearly succeeded in becoming
patriarch. In that year Babowai was caught engaged
in treasonable correspondence with the Roman Emperor Zeno. He was charged with writing that 'God
Dc

has delivered us up to an impious sovereign.' He may have done so, as he disliked King Peroz because Peroz favoured Barsumas, and also because he had suffered two years' imprisonment by Peroz on the ground that he was an apostate from Zoroastrianism. On the other hand, it may be that Barsumas was himself partly responsible for the charge being formulated.[1] In any case, the letter cost Babowai his life, and he was hanged by his fingers until he died. Barsumas now seized his opportunity, and called a synod to meet at Beth Lapat (Jundishapur).[2] This synod exalted 'Theodore the Interpreter' (Theodore of Mopsuestia) as the fount of true doctrine, and condemned the teaching of the Church in the Roman Empire. The synod was therefore absolutely Nestorian in character, and if its decisions had stood, 484 could be given as the definite date when the Persian Church became officially Nestorian. But, as will soon be seen, the power of this synod was only transient. In addition to doctrinal pronouncements, the synod of Beth Lapat discountenanced laws of celibacy. It declared marriage lawful for all, including priests and bishops. Barsumas gave a practical lead by marrying a nun.

Just as Barsumas, through this synod, seemed to have gained a decided ascendancy, King Peroz died. The new King, Balash (484–488), who exercised his right of appointing the new patriarch, passed over Barsumas

---

[1] Labourt, *Le Christianisme dans l'empire perse*, p. 142.
[2] There is some uncertainty as to whether this synod was convened shortly before or shortly after the death of Babowai. In either case the date was probably 484, though Eduard Meyer gives 483 (*Encyclopædia Britannica*, xvii. 585).

and appointed Acacius (485–496). Barsumas indignantly refused to acknowledge him. But Acacius had both religious and civil authority on his side, and at a synod held at Beth Adrai in 485, Barsumas had to submit. This synod declared that everything done at Beth Lapat was void, and the Beth Lapat synod of 484 has consequently no place in the canons of the Persian Church. Nevertheless, at the synod at Beth Adrai a confession was drawn up which definitely savoured of Nestorianism, and the abolition of celibacy was maintained. Acacius held another synod the following year (486) at Seleucia, where monophysitism was specifically condemned and the abolition of celibacy was reaffirmed. Although the condemnation of monophysitism ranked the Persians in that particular with the churches of the West, it does not really indicate the slightest change of attitude, for Nestorianism lies equally far from Western orthodoxy in the exactly opposite direction; so the condemnation of monophysitism by Nestorians is of no significance: it is exactly what would be expected.

But Acacius was evidently more a man of policy than of principle, for when a year or two later he was sent on an embassy to Constantinople he declared that he was not a Nestorian, had only intended to condemn monophysitism, and was willing to excommunicate Barsumas. His readiness to implement this willingness by action was not, however, put to the test, for on his return from Constantinople Barsumas was dead, murdered by monks, according to Barhebræus,[1] with

[1] Fortescue, op. cit., p. 82.

the keys of their cells. This was about 493. Acacius did not survive much longer, dying in 496.

He was succeeded by Babai (497–502). Soon after his accession Babai held two synods, in 498 and 499, at which the moderate policy of Acacius was abandoned and a return was made to the attitude of the synod convened by Barsumas at Beth Lapat in 484. Babai frankly accepted Nestorian theology, which thus became the official doctrine of the Persian Church; he went further than Barsumas and Acacius in the matter of the abolition of celibacy, allowing not only all bishops and priests to marry, but permitting re-marriage in the event of a wife's death; and he reasserted the right of the bishop of Seleucia-Ctesiphon to the title Patriarch of the East, declaring himself independent in every way of the churches of the Roman Empire and the rest of Christendom generally.

The position taken by Babai is perfectly unambiguous, and from his accession the Persian Church is not only definitely schismatical but professedly heretical.[1] From 497 we may therefore correctly refer to it as the Nestorian Church, and to its head as the Nestorian Patriarch. As will be seen shortly, the Nestorian Church extended far beyond the limits of the Persian Empire, and at one period the Nestorian Patriarch had a bigger area under his spiritual jurisdiction than any other Christian hierarch.

[1] For the connotation of these terms see p. 15.

CHAPTER III

THE NESTORIAN CHURCH IN THE TIME OF BABAI

497-502

ALTHOUGH Babai must have been a man of considerable practical ability to have been able to establish the
Persian Church on such a clearly defined basis, he was
a man of little culture, possibly unable even to read.[1]
He was, therefore, hardly competent to deal with
theological matters except in the most general way.
This deficiency, however, was remedied by Narses.
Narses was reckoned a great authority by the Nestorians, and did much toward defining their theological
positions at the critical time when they were setting
out into doctrinal as well as administrative isolation.
He had been a friend of Barsumas, and had been
associated with him in the work of the school at
Nisibis, eventually becoming its president. That
office he retained till his death in 507.

His teaching was quite definitely Nestorian, as is
evidenced by his extant poems and sermons. He left
no doubt as to the fount of Nestorian theology, describ-
ing Diodorus, Theodore, and Nestorius as the 'Three

[1] Fortescue, *Lesser Eastern Churches*, p. 82.

53

Doctors.' He vigorously defended the reputation of Nestorius, and ascribed his downfall to the bribery resorted to by his enemies, notably Cyril. He was, naturally, anti-monophysite, and declared Christ to have been incarnate in 'two natures, two persons, and one presence.'[1] This has been the Nestorian formula ever since, and crystallizes their heresy. Narses was so highly esteemed by the Nestorians that they styled him the 'Harp of the Holy Ghost.' The Jacobites,[2] however, refer to him as Narses the Leper.

It may now be desirable to see what was the extent of the Nestorian Patriarch's jurisdiction. It has already been stated that the patriarchate of the East was formed by the action of the Persian bishops at the synod of Markabta in 424, when they declared Seleucia-Ctesiphon no longer merely a catholicate but a patriarchate, and thus detached from the patriarchate of Antioch all those churches whose linkage with Antioch had been through the Catholicus of Seleucia-Ctesiphon. This involved nearly every church in the

---

[1] In the Syriac, 'two kyane, two knume, one parsufa,' which corresponds with the Greek ' δύο φύσεις, δύο ὑποστάσεις, ἓν πρόσωπον.' But it seems safe to assume that *parsufa* means no more than the appearance of unity presented externally by the fact of Jesus Christ having one body, one voice – in a word, one physical presence, a mere mask (a frequent meaning of πρόσωπον) of unification to cover the two personalities; and that *knuma* corresponds with ὑπόστασις in the sense of the person as an individuality, not in the sense of the nature of the person. The matter is not a simple one, and is carefully discussed by Bethune-Baker, *Nestorius and his Teaching*, pp. 212–232, or more shortly by Fortescue, op. cit., pp. 67–69, 84–85.

[2] A sect representing monophysitism in the East. They originated with Jacob Baradai in the sixth century, and with headquarters at Antioch had a number of churches in Syria and Persia. They were never so widely diffused as the Nestorians, and are represented to-day by a few small communities, mostly near Mosul, Mardin and Diarbekr.

continent of Asia with the exception of those within the boundaries of the Roman Empire. Whether some of the more remote churches realized that happenings at Seleucia-Ctesiphon during the fifth century had involved them in schism and heresy is open to question; but as they continued to look to the Patriarch of Seleucia-Ctesiphon as their spiritual head, from 497 all such churches must be reckoned as Nestorian churches.

The ways in which Christianity had reached these places fall outside the scope of the present work, but it is necessary to indicate the general limits of the area covered, and to give the names of the principal sees. This may most conveniently be done under broad geographical headings.

(1) The Persian Empire.

By far the greater number of the churches in the Nestorian patriarchate were situated in and near the valleys of the Tigris and Euphrates, that is, in the western part of the Persian Empire. In this region the churches were well organized, the Patriarch of Seleucia-Ctesiphon having under him a number of metropolitans, who supervised the bishops of the towns and villages in their provinces. If the plan followed in the Roman Empire had been adopted, the provinces of the metropolitans would have corresponded with the secular provinces. This, however, does not appear to have been the case, nor did the provinces of the metropolitans by any means cover the whole area of the patriarchate; for in addition to the metropolitan provinces there were many bishoprics independent of any metropolitan, whose immediate superior was the patriarch himself.

It is not an easy matter to discover the location and grouping of the various bishoprics. The facts have mostly to be gathered from the material collected by Assemani and Le Quien,[1] which is often difficult to interpret. This is because of the peculiar forms in which many of the names occur, making it difficult to recognize them, and because the same place sometimes appears again under a different name. Again, the sites of some of the obscurer places are difficult or impossible to identify. It is also often uncertain when the status of metropolitan was assumed by certain bishops; and when the status was assumed, it seems sometimes to have been more as a title of dignity than as indicative of jurisdiction, because some of those styled metropolitan do not appear to have had any bishops under them. Consequently, those who have endeavoured to compile lists of bishoprics seldom agree, and authorities like Wiltsch, Sachau and Kidd do not even agree as to the number of metropolitans at a given period. The following list, therefore, must be taken as provisional, being an attempt to interpret the data as carefully as possible. Considerations of space preclude detailed reasons for the conclusions reached.

At the time of Babai there were seven metropolitan provinces within the Persian Empire. It will readily be seen from the map on p. 58 that with the exception of Merv all these were in the Tigris-Euphrates area.

[1] In *Bibliotheca Orientalis* and *Oriens Christianus* respectively.

The following is a list of these metropolitan provinces together with their known dependent bishoprics:

Seat of the Patriarch: Seleucia-Ctesiphon.

(1) Province of Patriarchalis. Metropolitan at Kaskar, a bishop at Hira.

(2) Province of Nisibis. Metropolitan at Nisibis, a bishop at Bakerda.

(3) Province of Teredon. Metropolitan at Basrah, a bishop probably at Destesana, and a church, if not a bishopric, at Nahar-al-Marah.

(4) Province of Adiabene. Metropolitan at Erbil, bishops at Honita and Maalta.

(5) Province of Garamæa. Metropolitan at Karkha, bishops at Sciaarchadata and Dakuka.

(6) Province of Khurasan. Metropolitan at Merv.

(7) Province of Atropatene. Metropolitan at Taurisium.

Of the bishoprics owning direct allegiance to Seleucia-Ctesiphon, one important group was in the province of Susiana, and comprised the four bishoprics of Jundishapur, Susa, Ahwaz and Suster. Shortly afterwards (522) this group constituted a metropolitan province, with the bishop of Jundishapur as metropolitan. Three other bishoprics which a little later became centres of metropolitan provinces were Rawardshir, Rai and Herat. Other bishoprics not yet under metropolitans included Maiperkat, Nineveh, Singara, Drangerda, Ispahan and Nishapur. There was also a bishop for the province of Segestan, south of Herat.

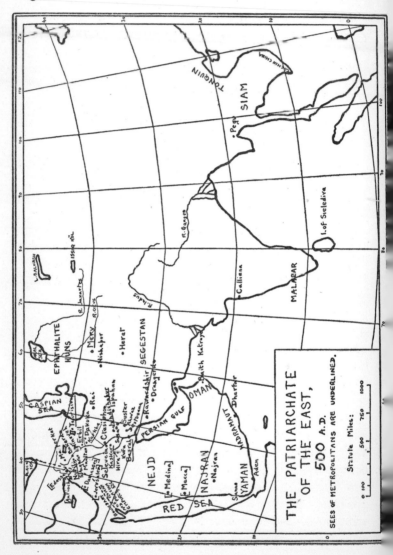

THE PATRIARCHATE
OF THE EAST,
500 A.D.

SEES OF METROPOLITANS ARE UNDERLINED.

Statute Miles:

In addition to these bishoprics there were a few monasteries (see pp. 73–74), and there were clergy schools at Seleucia, Dorkena and Erbil, as well as the famous one at Nisibis. Christianity was therefore widely diffused in Persia, being strongest in the western part.

(ii) *Arabia.*

Outside the Persian Empire the churches in the patriarchate were fewer and weaker, and our information about them is more scanty and uncertain. But it is generally agreed that Christianity had gained entrance to Arabia by this time. One of the most important modes of entrance had been by emigration of Christians from Persia in times of persecution, particularly during the latter part of the reign of Shapur II (310–379), who severely persecuted the Persian Church from about 339 onwards. These emigrants had mostly gone either by land through the semi-independent Arab state of Hira, or across the Persian Gulf to the coast of Oman, and thence south-westward to Hadramaut, Yaman, and Najran.

By the fifth century there were, therefore, many Christians in the southern half of the Arabian peninsula. There was, as already noted, a bishop at Hira under the Metropolitan of Kaskar, and there were bishops at Kufa, Beth Raman, Perath Messenes, Baith Katraye, and Najran. There were churches, and therefore probably bishops also, at Sana, Aden, and Dhafar; and there were monasteries and schools at Mathota and Jemana. Many tribes are named as having become Christian, including the Hamyar,[1] Ghassan, Rabia, Taglib, Bahra, Tonuch, part of the tribes of Tay and Kodaa, some tribes in the Nejd, the Beni Harith of Najran, and some other tribes between Kufa and Medina.

Although the evidence in some of these cases may be slender, and it is a matter of opinion how much of it we accept,[2] it is nevertheless sufficiently certain that the Christian element in Arabia was considerable; and because many of them were emigrants from Persia or descendants of such emigrants, and because political and geographical considerations linked them more naturally with Persia than with the Roman Empire, these Christians looked to the patriarch of Seleucia-Ctesiphon as their spiritual head. By virtue of that allegiance, therefore, these Arabian Christians must be reckoned in the Nestorian Church from 497 onwards.

(iii) *India*.

The extent of Christianity in India at the beginning of the sixth century is rather difficult to determine. Although some modern writers are to be found who think even St. Thomas the Apostle may have visited India, most ancient references must be received with caution, not only because the writers may have been quoting on doubtful evidence, but also because the

---

[1] *The Book of the Himyarites*, Syriac fragments collected and translated by Axel Moberg in 1934, has gone far towards proving that Christianity was more widely diffused in south Arabia than had formerly been supposed.

[2] Stewart, for example, accepts most of it; Assemani, Sale, and Zwemer much of it; and Harnack very little. For much of the evidence see Cheikho, *Le Christianisme en Arabie avant l'Islam*.

name India was very loosely used, being sometimes applied even to Arabia Felix or Ethiopia. It is also possible that after some centuries a confusion arose between St. Thomas the Apostle and Thomas of Jerusalem (Thomas Cannaneo), who quite probably visited south-west India in the fourth century. The persistent Thomas tradition in India may, therefore, be a genuine one, but its basis of reality may be the work of Thomas of Jerusalem rather than that of the Apostle.

But it is safe to say that there were certainly some Christian communities in India at this time, and an indication of their locations may be gathered from the writings[1] of Cosmas Indicopleustes, who wrote about 530. He says there were bishops at Calliana (near Bombay), in Male (Malabar), in the island of Sielediva (Ceylon), and in the island of Taprobana in the Indian Ocean; and that there were Christians in Pegu, the Ganges valley, Cochin China, Siam, and Tonquin. He definitely states that they were ecclesiastically dependent upon Persia, so what Christians there may have been in these regions must be reckoned as Nestorians from the sixth century.

(iv) Turkestan.[2]

Persian Christian missionaries had begun to make converts among the Ephthalite Huns and the Turks in

---

[1] *Topographia Christiana.*

[2] A convenient name for a region of Central Asia extending approximately from the Caspian Sea to Lake Baikal. Historically the area to which the name has been applied has varied considerably. That portion between the rivers Oxus and Jaxartes is often referred to as Transoxiana, and contains the important towns of Samarqand and Bukhara.

the neighbourhood of the Oxus, but no great impression
had been made so early as 497.   In the following year,
however, when King Kavadh I had to flee temporarily
from Persia into Turkestan because of the success of
the usurper Djamasp, he was accompanied on his
journey by the bishop of Arran,[1] together with four
presbyters and two laymen, who were going on a
mission into the same region.[2]   This mission of the
year 498 was very successful, and many Turks became
Christians.   The presbyters continued their work for
seven years, but the laymen remained until 530.

In addition to the work of missionaries, Christian
influence was making its way into the same region
through the agency of Christian doctors, scribes, and
artisans, who were readily able to find employment
among a people of a lower culture.

(v) *China.*

It is doubtful whether there were any Christian
communities in China so early as A.D. 500.   Christian
influences, perhaps mainly through Gnostic and
Manichæan channels, had already affected Chinese
thought to some small extent,[3] and there may have
been sporadic missionary effort even so early as A.D.
300.[4]   But the founding of Christian churches did not

---

[1] Possibly the region of that name immediately north of Atropatene
and a little to the west of the Caspian Sea.   But it may be doubted
whether there were bishops of Arran so early as this.   Quite possibly
Arran should here be taken as one of the many variants of Herat
(see p. 224).

[2] Mingana, *Bulletin of the John Rylands Library*, ix. 303.

[3] See A. Lloyd's article, 'Gnosticism in Japan,' in *The East and the
West*, April 1910.

[4] Thomas of Marga, *Historia Monastica.*

take place, at least on any effective scale, till the Nestorian missionary expansion of the seventh and eighth centuries.

This survey of non-Roman Asiatic Christianity at the end of the fifth century shows that Babai had assumed the spiritual headship of churches scattered over an area stretching from Arabia in the west to India in the east. The map on p. 58 shows not only their distribution, but indicates that their real strength was in the Tigris-Euphrates area. Elsewhere they were sparser, and our knowledge of them is correspondingly less sure. Nevertheless, these churches certainly comprised a considerable body of Christians, whose future history is that of the Nestorian Church.

CHAPTER IV

THE NESTORIAN CHURCH UNDER THE SASSANIDS

502–651

1. RELATION TO THE STATE

DURING the next one and a half centuries the Nestorian Church steadily consolidated its position in Persia and in the regions immediately adjoining. The Sassanid dynasty[1] continued in power, and was, on the whole, tolerant. This was because it was recognized that the Church in Persia was alienated from the Church of the Roman Empire, and it was considered more prudent to make Christians within the Persian Empire feel secure within their national boundaries, rather than to encourage them to look to their co-religionists across the border. The status conferred upon Persian Christians by Yazdegerd I (p. 46) was therefore generally respected.

Nevertheless, there was occasional persecution. This usually arose at times when there was tension or war between the Roman and Persian empires. In such circumstances, as the conflict was between an empire avowedly Christian and an empire officially

[1] For a list of the Sassanid Kings, with indications of their attitude toward Christianity, see pp. 81–82.

Zoroastrian,[1] Christians in Persia were not unnaturally suspect. It was feared that their sympathies might be with the enemy on account of their religion, and that spies and plotters might reasonably be looked for among them. In addition, the Magians, as the leaders of Zoroastrianism, were not adverse to encouraging repressive measures against the members of a rival faith when other circumstances made such repressive measures seem reasonable.

One such persecution during this period was in the reign of Chosroes I (531–579), and coincided with the time during which he was at war with the Roman Empire, 540–545.[2] Among the victims of this persecution was the good Patriarch Mar Aba I (see pp. 71–72). He was arrested and imprisoned, but was offered his freedom if he would promise to make no more converts. This he refused to do, and continued in prison for a considerable time. It is said that the hard treatment he received during his imprisonment hastened his death, though he lived till 552, seven years after this

[1] Zoroastrianism (Mazdæism) was the dominant religion of Persia from about the eighth century B.C. until the fall of the Sassanid dynasty in A.D. 651. It is named after Zoroaster (Zarathustra), whose date is very uncertain, but who may have flourished about 1000 B.C. Zoroaster established a religious system based on the old Iranian folk-religion, but formulating it as a definite dualism. The supreme power of good is Ahura Mazda (later contracted to Ormazd), and the supreme power of evil is Ahriman. The moral and ethical tone of the religion is a high one, the teaching being embodied in their sacred book the Avesta. The erroneous idea that Zoroastrians were fire worshippers arose from the large place occupied by fire in their sacred symbolism. The priesthood was restricted to the members of an exclusive caste, known as the Magians.

[2] This was the period of actual warfare, and although an armistice was concluded in 545 the war continued spasmodically for some years, chiefly in Lazica (Colchis), until a fifty years' peace was concluded in 562.

persecution had ended. Apart from this one period
of persecution, Chosroes I seems to have been quite
tolerant.

Another outbreak occurred towards the end of the
reign of Chosroes II (590–628). The reasons on this
occasion were of the same general nature as previously,
with the added motive of an urgent necessity for raising
money. To show how Persia was reduced to such a
pass necessitates a brief description of the course of
events during the reign of Chosroes II. Though
Chosroes may have been unwise, he was also unfortunate, and was beset with difficulties from the very
beginning. Two pretenders, Bahram Cobin and
Prince Bistam, endeavoured to displace him immediately he came to the throne, whereupon he fled to the
Romans and secured the help of the Emperor Maurice.
With his aid he eventually gained the upper hand,
though Bistam held out in Media till 596. Though
Maurice's aid had re-established Chosroes, it had cost
the cession of some Persian territory, and also implied
a certain dependence. When, therefore, Maurice was
assassinated in 602 by the usurper Phocas, Chosroes
saw an opportunity for regaining his lost prestige, and
on the pretext of avenging Maurice, made war against
the Roman Empire.

For several years everything went in his favour, and
for a time there seems to have been no prejudice
against Persian Christians. Indeed, the Patriarch
Sabaryeshu I (596–604) was with the Persian army in
603 in order that he might pray for its success. Chosroes
succeeded in reaching as far as Chalcedon, just opposite

Constantinople, and even occupied Egypt. Antioch
and Damascus fell under his sway, and he also captured
Jerusalem, taking away the Holy Cross. Meanwhile
he was becoming less complacent toward Christians.
Sabaryeshu had died in 604, and Gregory had become
patriarch in 605. But when Gregory died in 608,
Chosroes would not allow a new patriarch to be
appointed, and the see had to remain vacant till 628.
Although deprived of their official head, the Nestorians
were not leaderless, as during this period they were
admirably led by Mar Babai, abbot of the monastery
on Mount Izala, whose effective work in difficult circumstances is described later (pp. 74–75).

The successes of Chosroes continued from 602 till 622,
and if he had been able to consolidate his gains he would
have well deserved his title Parvez (Conqueror). But
in 622 the tide turned. The Emperor Heraclius, who
had come to power in 610, had gradually been bringing
order out of the chaotic state into which the Roman
Empire had fallen, and was at last ready to take action.
He invaded Persia and inflicted crushing defeats on
the armies of Chosroes. In 624 he destroyed the great
fire temple in Atropatene, and by 627 had penetrated
into the Tigris province. These disasters had the
usual unfortunate results for Persian Christians; already
out of favour, they now had to endure persecution.
This persecution was partly motived by the urgent
need for money to carry on the forlorn defence, for the
Christians had many men of substance among them.
Many innocent persons thus suffered to appease Persian
fear and to help refill the depleted treasury. The

most notable case was that of Yazdin, silversmith to the king, and a zealous Nestorian. Not only was he killed and his goods confiscated, but his wife was tortured to make her reveal any secret hoards. It is interesting to remark that the wife of Chosroes was herself a Nestorian, but her influence was evidently insufficient to avert the misfortunes which befell her fellow-Christians.

But the forces of Heraclius continued their steady advance, and Chosroes had to flee from Dastagerd to Ctesiphon. Revolution broke out, and in 628 Chosroes was deposed and killed by his son Kavadh II. His reign lasted only a few months, and after his death complete chaos ensued. During the next four years power was held by a succession of rulers, some of the Sassanid dynasty, others mere usurpers, till in 632 the magnates[1] united and gave the kingship to Yazdegerd III, a grandson of Chosroes II. Peace had been concluded with Heraclius, the Holy Cross had been returned, and the old frontiers had been restored, so that there might have been hope that the two empires would recover from their futile and exhausting wars.

But before Persia had time to recuperate, a new enemy was upon her. The great Arab expansion had begun, and by 633 incursions had already commenced into Persian territory. The Persian resistance was feeble, and a decisive defeat was inflicted on the Persians at Kadisiya in 637. This gave a large tract of territory, including the important twin cities of Seleucia and Ctesiphon, into the hands of the Arabs. Yazdegerd

---

[1] The influential Persian higher nobility.

held out in Media till 641, when he suffered another grave defeat at the battle of Nehavend. Thereafter he became practically a fugitive, till he was assassinated at Merv in 651. With the death of Yazdegerd III the Sassanid dynasty came to an end, and Persia was soon afterwards completely under the control of the Arabs.

Fortunately for the inhabitants of Persia, most of them belonged to faiths which were treated by Muslims with special tolerance. According to the teaching of Muhammad as recorded in the Koran, leniency was to be shown to Jews and Christians, on the ground that they were 'people of the Book' (the Bible), and to that extent had reverence for the true God. Although no mention is made of them in the Koran, in practice the same tolerance was extended toward Zoroastrians, presumably because the Avesta was regarded as a book similar to the Bible, and Ahura Mazda was identified with Allah, the one God. Little difference, therefore, was shown by the Arabs in their treatment of the two religions, Christianity and Zoroastrianism; nevertheless, the effect of the change of government was much more adversely felt by the Zoroastrians. This was because Zoroastrianism had owed so much of its influence to its standing as the national faith. That prestige was now gone, and it steadily declined as a live force in Persia. Indeed, it almost disappeared altogether from Persia, and to-day the only Persian Zoroastrians are a few families in Kerman and the oasis of Yezd. The residue of the faithful emigrated to India, where their descendants, now known as Parsees, maintain the

Zoroastrian faith. They number about 94,000, and are to be found mostly in the Bombay Presidency. In doctrine they have tended away from the original dualism toward monotheism.

Christianity, however, had nothing to lose in prestige, as it had long been secondary, from the official point of view, to Zoroastrianism. It made little difference that it should now be secondary to Islam. The Arab attitude was on the whole tolerant, partly, as already stated, because Christians were a 'people of the Book,' and partly because Muhammad is said to have at one time had a Nestorian teacher, Sergius Bahira.[1] This toleration continued, with occasional exceptions, for several centuries, and falls to be described in the next chapter.

2. INTERNAL CONDITION

In spite of the rivalry of Zoroastrianism, the official religion of the Persian Empire, and the occasional persecutions referred to above, this period was on the whole one of advance and development. Babai and his immediate successors in the patriarchate did not accomplish much of importance; but considerable advances were made toward the middle and end of the sixth century, when several men of outstanding character and ability arose in the Nestorian Church. Mention must be made of what each of these accomplished.

The most eminent Nestorian Patriarch of the

[1] Assemani, *Bibliotheca Orientalis*, III. ii. 94.

sixth century was Mar Aba I, who held office from 540
to 552. He was by birth and education a Zoroastrian,
being a member of the Magian clan, and before becoming a Christian had attained to the important position
of secretary to the governor of a Persian civil province.
The mode of his conversion is recorded in what we
can only regard as a legend. He was about to cross
the Tigris in a ferry, when he noticed a Jew named
Joseph in the boat. He ordered the Jew out of the
boat, telling him to make his crossing later. The
ferry, however, could not make headway, being twice
driven back by the wind. Mar Aba then allowed the
Jew on board, and the crossing was easily accomplished. He then discovered that the Jew was a
Christian, and being impressed both by the miraculous
event and by the humility and courtesy of Joseph, he
decided to give up his official position and ask for
baptism.

It may be that the substratum of fact under this
story is that Mar Aba became attracted to Christianity
by some signal act of kindness shown him by a Christian, or by his observation of the high standard of the
lives of many of them. Be that as it may, he became a
Christian, and went to the clergy school at Nisibis to
study. He visited Constantinople between 525 and
533, and admitted there his adherence to the teachings
of Theodore of Mopsuestia and to the Nestorian
Christology. He was made patriarch in 540, and did
much for the good order of the churches under his care.
During his time the ecclesiastical provinces were well
administered, he himself making many personal visits

to the various parts of his patriarchate, so that irregu-
larities and abuses might be put down.   In particular he stopped the practice of incest, a Persian vice
which some of the Christians were beginning to copy.
In addition to such reforms he helped to establish new
churches.   The churches at Anbar and Karkha[1] in the
province of Patriarchalis date from his time; so does
the church on the island of Ormuz in the Persian Gulf,
which belonged to the province of Fars; and the
Nestorian church which existed for a time at Edessa.

Altogether, Mar Aba did much to strengthen the
Persian Church, and he is praised even by Roman
Catholic writers, whose commendation of heretics is
obviously likely to be very restrained.   It is significant,
therefore, that Fortescue[2] feels able to say of him that
'but for his doubtful attitude about the heresy [i.e.
Nestorianism], he was in every way an excellent
prelate,' and that Labourt[3] styles him 'A glorious con-
fessor of the Faith, the light of the Persian Church, to
which he left the double treasure of blameless doctrine
and a model life.'   It is also to be remembered that
much of his work had to be accomplished during the
time of persecution under Chosroes I, to which reference has been made above (p. 65).   His work was
carried on with almost equal efficiency by his successor
Joseph (552–567).   During his time there arose a
church at Naamania in the province of Patriarchalis,
and one at Zuabia in the province of Adiabene.

[1] In Babylonia.   Not the same as the Karkha in the province of
Garamæa, p. 57.   It is not heard of again.
[2] *Lesser Eastern Churches*, p. 83.
[3] *Le Christianisme dans l'empire perse*, p. 191.

At about the same time that Mar Aba and Joseph were so capably governing the Persian Church, a far-reaching influence was also being exerted by Abraham of Kaskar. Abraham, who was born about 491, revived monasticism in Persia. During the third and fourth centuries there had been monastic orders in Persia, but during the latter part of the fifth century and the earlier part of the sixth there had been a movement away from all that monastic life implies, a movement considerably accelerated by the general relaxation of the Church's teaching on celibacy (pp. 50–52). Abraham, after first studying at Nisibis, went to Egypt, and was so impressed by the flourishing monastic life he saw there that he decided to return to his own land and endeavour to restore Persian monasticism to an equally well ordered condition. On his return he established or restored the monastery on Mount Izala near Nisibis, and soon gathered round himself a great company of monks living to a stricter rule than had lately been customary in Persia. From that time the monastery on Mount Izala was the most influential religious house in the Nestorian Church, and its abbot often came second only to the patriarch in influence and power.

Abraham's example at Mount Izala led to the establishment of many new monasteries and to the reform of those which had continued to exist in a lax form. Details of Abraham's life and work, and of the rules he made for Persian monasticism, may be found in Thomas of Marga's *Historia Monastica* (*The Book of Governors*). The rules were very similar to those followed in Egypt.   The monks wore tunic, belt, cloak, hood, and sandals, and carried a cross and stick.   Their tonsure was distinctive, being cruciform.   At first they met for common prayer seven times a day, but later this was reduced to four times.   They were vegetarians, and ate only once a day, at noon.   Celibacy, of course, was rigidly enforced.   Those who were more capable engaged in study and the copying of books, while others worked on the land.   After three years a monk could, if the abbot agreed, retire to absolute solitude as a hermit.   The connexion between the monasteries and the bishops was closer than was usual in the West, the control of monastic property being in the hands of the nearest bishop.   This no doubt both strengthened and enriched the hierarchy.[1]

From this time onwards monasticism continued to be a considerable force in the Nestorian Church, and produced some of its greatest men.   A list of some of the more important monasteries may conveniently be given here: Mount Izala near Nisibis, Dorkena near Seleucia (for many centuries the burial place of the patriarchs), Tela, Baxaja, Haigla, Henda, Zarnucha, Camula, Anbar, Beth-Zabda, Chuchta, Kuph. Abraham died in 586 at the venerable age of ninety-five, having lived long enough to see great results from his labours and example.   He was succeeded as abbot by Dadyeshu.

One of the greatest sons of the monastery on Mount Izala was Mar Babai the Great (569–628).   (This Babai is to be carefully distinguished from the patriarch

[1] Fortescue, *Lesser Eastern Churches*, p. 112.

Babai.) Originally a monk at the Mount Izala monastery, he subsequently became abbot, probably succeeding Dadyeshu. He was a strength to the Nestorian Church at a very difficult period, acting as its administrative head during the long vacancy after the death of Gregory in 608 till the appointment of Yeshuyab II in 628 (see p. 67). In spite of the difficulties of the times, or perhaps because fear and uncertainty turned more people toward religion, many new churches were established in his time: two in the province of Patriarchalis, Sena and Badraia; two in the province of Nisibis, Balada and Arzun; one in the province of Garamæa, Marangerd; and one at Beth-Daron in Mesopotamia. In addition to administrative work he helped to establish Nestorian doctrine on a well-defined basis, and his *Book of the Union* (i.e. of Godhead and manhood in Christ) is still accepted as a true statement of the Nestorian position. He exalts Diodorus, Theodore, and Nestorius, and rejects the Council of Chalcedon and the term Theotokos. He also inveighs against monophysites and Henanians,[1] which shows that Jacobites and other sects and factions did not leave the Nestorian Church undisturbed.

After Mar Babai's death in 628 it was possible to appoint a patriarch again, and Yeshuyab II (628–643) was instated. Despite the troublous times in which he had to labour, he appears to have undertaken

---

[1] A party within the Nestorian Church, followers of Hanana, who was head of the school at Nisibis in the sixth century. They accepted the Council of Chalcedon, and preferred the teaching of Chrysostom to that of Theodore of Mopsuestia. They may perhaps be regarded as pro-Catholic Nestorians.

his duties effectively, and was responsible for the sending of a mission to China (see p. 130).

3. NESTORIAN CHURCHES OUTSIDE PERSIA

(i) *Arabia.*

Christianity made little further advance in Arabia after the beginning of the sixth century. Its only notable success was at Hira, where, according to the *Book of the Himyarites*,[1] Mundhar, phylarch (petty king) of the Arabs in Hira, became a Christian in 512, and was baptized by Simon, bishop of Hira. The king's sister, Henda, was also baptized, and founded a cœnobium (convent).[2] Apart from this, the principal event which affected Arabian Christianity was the struggle between Najran and Yaman. There were many Jews in Arabia, and they seem to have been particularly influential in Yaman. Indeed, Masruq Dhu Namas (or Dunaas), king of Yaman, is supposed to have been himself a Jew. But in Najran Christianity predominated, so that when war broke out between Yaman and Najran in 519, religious differences added to the bitterness of the struggle.

As in the wars between the Roman and Persian empires, the political clash brought with it the tendency to persecute in each country the minority who subscribed to the faith of the majority in the country of the

[1] See p. 60, footnote.
[2] The authority for these statements is Amrus, a Nestorian. Barhebræus, however, a Jacobite, asserts that the conversion was made by Jacobites.

enemy. Thus Christians began to be persecuted in Yaman, and Jews in Najran. Christians set fire to synagogues, and Masruq burned Christian churches. He slew numbers of Christians, particularly in Dhafar, Hadramaut, and Najran, which he had succeeded in subjugating. The persecution was fiercest about the year 500.[1]

In 525, however, the Abyssinians came to the aid of the Christians, King Elesbaan (or Kaleb) leading his army in person. He completely defeated the forces of Masruq, who, seeing that his power was broken, drowned himself in the Red Sea. Elesbaan only stayed in Arabia seven months, but before returning to Abyssinia he set up a Himyarite noble as Christian ruler in Najran and Yaman. The dynasty thus instituted continued in power until the time of Muhammad, though with Persian help Masruq's successors were able to regain Yaman. But Yaman may have again come under the sway of these Christian rulers, for in 567 Abraha Ashram is described as Christian king of Yaman, and as building a new cathedral at Sana. The new cathedral was defiled by some pagan Arabs from the north, and Abraha in 568 led a punitive expedition against Mecca. The Koreish Arabs, however, easily repulsed him, and their victory is celebrated in Sura 105 of the Koran. It has been suggested that Abraha's defeat was partly due to the outbreak of an epidemic among his troops, possibly small-pox.

Christianity in Arabia had not now many years

---

[1] For details see the *Book of the Himyarites*, or extensive quotations from it in Stewart, *Nestorian Missionary Enterprise*, pp. 56–65.

before it, for about this time, probably in 569, Muhammad was born. After 622, the year of his flight (Arabic *hegira*) from Mecca to Medina, from which momentous event the Muhammadan era is dated, he gradually gained power over the greater part of Arabia, and before his death in 632 he had already planned the extension of his faith and dominion into Syria and Persia. Although the harshness of Muhammad and his followers toward peoples who refused to accept his faith has sometimes been exaggerated, there is no doubt that far less toleration was shown in Arabia itself than elsewhere. Muhammad is supposed to have left the dying command that 'Throughout the peninsula there shall be no second creed.' Whether he actually said so or not, his successors acted on the assumption that he had, and a determined attempt was made to eradicate all religions but Islam[1] from Arabia. Partly by massacres and stern repressive measures, partly by defections to Islam prompted by fear or policy, this ideal had been very nearly realized by the time of the fourth caliph, Ali (656–661). After his time traces of Christianity in Arabia are very meagre, and by the end of the seventh century it had ceased to be a force of any importance in the peninsula.

(ii) *India*.

Apart from the evidence of Cosmas Indicopleustes given above (p. 61), there is little specific mention of

[1] The religious system formulated by Muhammad is correctly known as Islam (Arabic *submission*, i.e. to God), and those who follow it are Muslims (Arabic *those who submit*). The terms Muhammadanism and Muhammadan are not really good usage, but will occasionally be employed when connexion with Muhammad himself needs stressing.

the Indian churches during this period. Nevertheless, we have no reason to suppose that such Christian communities as there were did not continue steadily, if uneventfully, with their work and witness. Two interesting inscribed crosses probably date from this period. One was found at Milapur (now known as St. Thomas's Mount) near Madras in 1547, and is usually called the Thomas Cross, and another at Kotayam (Travancore). Both bear inscriptions in ancient Persian (Pahlavi).[1]

(iii) *Turkestan*.

There is little to record as to the progress of the Nestorian Church in this region between the expedition under the bishop of Arran (p. 62), and the renewed missionary activity in the time of the patriarch Timothy I (p. 128).

(iv) *China*.

The first Nestorian mission to China of which we have any authentic record was sent by the patriarch Yeshuyab II (628–643) just before the close of this period. In order to avoid an unnecessary break of continuity, the account of it will be reserved to the next period (p. 130).

---

[1] Robinson, *History of Christian Missions*, p. 65.

BISHOPS, CATHOLICI, AND PATRIARCHS OF
SELEUCIA-CTESIPHON, 315–660

(This list is based on Kidd's collation[1] of the data given by
Assemani and Labourt)

Papa Bar Aggai, *floruit circa* 315.
Simon Bar Sabæ, *obiit* 341.[2]
Sadhost, 341–342.[3]
Barbasemin, 342–346.
VACANT, 346–383.
Tomarsa, 383–392.
Qayoma, 395–399.
Isaac, 399–410.[4]   (First Catholicus, 410.)
Ahai, 410–415.
Yaballaha I, 415–420.
Maanes (Mana), 420.
Marabochtus (Farbokt), 421.
Dadyeshu, 421–456.   (First Patriarch, 424.)
Babowai, 457–484.
Acacius, 485–496.[5]
Babai, 497–502.[6]
Silas, 505–523.
Narses and
Elisæus, 524–539.
Paulus, 539.

[1] *Churches of Eastern Christendom*, p. 416.
[2] Fortescue, *Lesser Eastern Churches*, gives *ob.* 339.
[3] For variants in the spelling of this and other names, see the supplemental index, p. 226.
[4] On this date, see the note on p. 44.
[5] Wiltsch, *Geography and Statistics of the Church*, gives 486–496.
[6] This date is generally given as 497–502/3, and is so given by Kidd. Wiltsch gives 498–502/3.

Mar Aba I, 540–552.

Joseph, 552–567.

Ezechiel, 570–581.

Yeshuyab I, 582–595.

Sabaryeshu I, 596–604.

Gregory, 605–608.[1]

VACANT, 608–628.

Yeshuyab II, 628–643.

Maremes, 647–650.

Yeshuyab III, 650–660.[2]

THE SASSANID KINGS OF PERSIA

(with indications of their attitude to Christianity)

Ardashir (Artaxerxes) I, 224–241.

Shapur (Sapor) I, 241–272.

Hormizd I, 272–273.

Bahram I, 273–276.

Bahram II, 276–293.

Bahram III, 293.

Narses, 293–302.

Hormizd II, 302–310.

Shapur II, 310–379. First Persian king to persecute Christians. Began a fierce persecution in 339, which continued throughout his reign. Many thousands perished. Many Christians emigrated.

[1] Wiltsch gives 616 instead of 608, the vacancy 616–633, and Yeshuyab II, 632[sic]–653.

[2] Wiltsch gives 655–664. *Encyclopædia Britannica*, xxi. 724, gives 647–657/8.

Ardashir II, 379–383.	Continued the persecution, but less fiercely.
Shapur III, 383–388.	Comparatively tolerant.
Bahram IV, 388–399.	Comparatively tolerant.
Yazdegerd I, 399–420.	Very tolerant. Gave Christians a recognized status (see p. 46).
Bahram V, 420–438.	Persecution 420–422. Afterwards tolerant.
Yazdegerd II, 438–457.	Fairly tolerant, except for a fierce persecution in 448, when thousands perished, principally at Karkha.
Hormizd III, 457–459.	
Peroz, 457–484.	Persecution in 465 against non-Nestorian Christians.
Balash, 484–488.	
Kavadh I, 488–531.	Tolerant.
(Djamasp, 496–498, usurper.)	
Chosroes I, 531–579.	Persecution 540–545. Otherwise tolerant.
Hormizd IV, 579–590.	Tolerant. Ordered Zoroastrians and Christians to dwell peaceably together.
Chosroes II, 590–628.	At first tolerant. Intolerant after 608.
Kavadh II, 628.	
Ardashir III, 628–630.	
Period of unsettlement: Shahrbaraz, Boran and others, 630–632.	
Yazdegerd III, 632–651.	

CHAPTER V

THE NESTORIAN CHURCH UNDER THE
CALIPHATE
651–1258

I. RELATION TO THE STATE

THE Arab conquest of Persia had naturally caused
suffering to the Christian element in the population.
But this cannot be called persecution, because it was
simply the inevitable concomitant of invasion. Once
the Arabs had become established, the Christians were
certainly no worse off than they had been previously.
The empire of the Sassanids now became part of the
Arabian Empire, which by the end of the seventh
century extended from the shores of the Mediterranean
and Red Seas to the Oxus and the Indus, and from the
Indian Ocean to the Caucasus and the Caspian. This
empire is usually described as the Caliphate, being
ruled by the successors (Arabic *khalifah*, successor) of
Muhammad. The first four caliphs, the immediate
successors of Muhammad, are known as the perfect
caliphs (632–661). Then followed thirteen caliphs of
the Umayyad dynasty (661–749), and lastly thirty-
seven caliphs of the Abbasid dynasty (749–1258).[1]

[1] For a list of the caliphs, see pp. 139–140.

During the whole period Mecca and Medina remained the Holy Cities of Islam, but the political centre, originally at Medina, moved first to Damascus and finally to Baghdad.

After the death of the caliph Mutawakkil in 861 the Caliphate began both to decay and to change its character. Disorders and rebellions within and Turkish incursions from across the Oxus reduced both its territory and power, until finally the Caliphs became mere titular religious figureheads, 'content with sermon and coin,'[1] and the real power was in the hands of the Turks. The most notable Turkish leaders at this period belonged to the Seljuk family of the Ghuzz tribe. These Seljuks gradually asserted their dominance, gaining control of Merv by 1040 and of Baghdad by 1055. From the latter date it is not incorrect to say that a Seljuk dynasty was in real control of what had once been the Caliphate, though it is to be remembered that the Seljuks were Muslims, and that they still conceded to the Abbasid caliphs the spiritual headship of the State. This was the state of affairs when the Mongol expansion of the thirteenth century took place; and the last Abbasid caliph of Baghdad, Mustasim, was murdered when the Mongol Hulagu captured Baghdad in 1258. During this period of over six centuries the official religion of the Caliphate was Islam, and it is now necessary to trace its attitude to Christianity.

[1] Quoted by M. J. de Goeje as a common saying regarding the caliphs from the time of Muti (946–974) onwards. (*Encyclopædia Britannica* (11th edition), v. 52.)

Muhammad himself seems at first to have regarded Christians with favour, but later his attitude became less conciliatory.   At first he evidently regarded Christians as likely to make good Muslims, if they would only renounce the tenets in their faith which he considered erroneous, these being particularly the divinity of Christ and the doctrine of the Trinity. Thus, until the last Suras of the Koran (last, that is, in time of composition, not as usually printed and numbered), he generally speaks kindly and hopefully of Christians.   It is to be noted that the expression 'people of the Book' in the passages quoted below includes both Christians and Jews, but the whole tone of the Koran is less friendly toward Jews than it is toward Christians.   The exact chronology of the Suras is still uncertain, but it is generally agreed that Sura 9 is among the last two or three.   It will, therefore, be sufficient to compare a few extracts from Suras acknowledged to be earlier with extracts from Sura 9.[1]

In Sura 98 we read[2]: 'But the unbelievers among the people of the Book, and among the polytheists,[3] shall go into the fire of Gehenna to abide therein for aye. Of all creatures they were the worst.   But they who believe and do the things that are right, these of all creatures are the best.'

[1] The quotations given are from Suras which are set in the same relative chronological order by Nöldeke, Grimm, Muir, and Rodwell, namely 98, 3, 57, 9.   The numbers by which the Suras are usually quoted have no relation to the times of their composition.

[2] Following Rodwell's translation, which is smoother, if less literal, than Palmer's.   The only place where Palmer differs from Rodwell except in phraseology will be noted.

[3] Palmer translates 'idolaters.'

In Sura 3: 'Among the people of the Book are those who believe in God, and in what He hath sent down to you, and in what He hath sent down to them, humbling themselves before God. They barter not the signs of God for a mean price. These! their recompense awaiteth them with their Lord: aye! God is swift to take account.'

In Sura 57: 'Of old sent we Noah and Abraham, and on their seed conferred the gift of prophecy, and the Book; and some of them we guided aright; but many were evil doers. Then we caused our apostles to follow in their footsteps; and we caused Jesus the son of Mary to follow them; and we gave them the Evangel, and we put into the hearts of those who followed him kindness and compassion. But as to the monastic life, they invented it themselves. The desire only of pleasing God did we prescribe to them, and this they observed not as it ought to have been observed. But to such of them as believed gave we their reward, though many of them were perverse.'

But in Sura 9, which is generally accepted as dating from shortly before Muhammad's death, the tone of conciliation is less evident, and Jews and Christians alike are regarded as enemies of Islam: 'The Jews say, "Ezra is a son of God"; and the Christians say, "The Messiah is a son of God." Such the sayings of their mouths! They resemble the sayings of the infidels of old! God do battle with them! How are they misguided! They take their teachers, and their monks, and the Messiah, son of Mary, for Lords beside God, though bidden to worship one God only. There is no

God but He! Far from His glory be what they associate with Him!'

In this Sura we also find justification for two principles which were often applied in later years, namely, to tax other peoples converted to Islam at a higher rate than Arab Muslims, and, sometimes, to tolerate communities of other faiths in return for special tribute: 'Kill those who join other gods with God wherever ye shall find them; and seize them, besiege them, and lay wait for them with every kind of ambush. But if they shall convert, and observe prayer, and pay the obligatory alms, then let them go their way, for God is gracious, merciful.' 'Make war upon such of those to whom the Scriptures have been given as believe not in God, or in the last day, and who forbid not that which God and His Apostle have forbidden, and who profess not the profession of the truth, until they pay tribute out of hand, and they be humbled.'

It is unfortunate that one of the Suras which contains important references to Christians is of disputed date. Nöldeke and Rodwell place Sura 5 later than Sura 9, while Grimm and Muir place it earlier. To fit in with the general argument advanced above we should wish to regard it as earlier. But in any case the relevant passages must be quoted: 'Verily, they who believe, and the Jews, and the Sabeites,[1] and the Christians – whoever of them believeth in God and in the last day, and doth what is right, on them shall come no fear,

___

[1] The Sabeites (Sabians, Sabæans) were a small semi-Christian sect who were to be found mostly near the mouth of the Euphrates. Ceremonial ablutions occupied a considerable place in their system.

neither shall they be put to grief.' 'If the people of the
Book believe and have the fear of God, we will surely
put away their sins from them, and will bring them into
gardens of delight.' 'Thou shalt certainly find those to
be nearest in affection to them [i.e. to those who
believe], who say, "We are Christians." This, because
some of them are priests and monks, and because they
are free from pride.'

Nevertheless, uncertainty about the date of Sura 5
does not vitiate the general trend of the evidence,
which is that Muhammad at first hoped that Jews and
Christians would become ready and valuable converts
to Islam; but that when experience brought disappointment his attitude toward them hardened.

Muhammad had died in 632, so that by the time the
Arabs had completed the conquest of Persia (651), a
certain amount of practical experience in dealing with
subject peoples who refused to accept Islam had been
gained. Apart from the occasional massacres which
ancient empire expansion always seemed to involve, it
is a travesty of Muhammadanism to say that the alter-
native was 'Islam or the sword.' It was only in Arabia
itself that a really determined effort was made to
eradicate every religion but Islam. Outside Arabia,
policy usually based itself upon the verses from Sura 9
quoted on p. 87. These were interpreted as permitting communities of unbelievers to continue to live, but
under conditions of special taxation and humiliation.
Such a community within the State is usually termed a
melet. But the melet system was not a Muslim innova-
tion, nor did it come as strange to the Persian

Christians. Their status under the Sassanids had been of a very similar nature ever since the synod of Seleucia in 410, when Yazdegerd I had given them recognition as a subject community within the State (p. 46). The conditions of extra taxation and other disabilities were also not new to them; Shapur II had made the Christians pay double taxes for his wars against the Romans, which had continued intermittently from 337 till 363, and Chosroes I (531–579) had levied an additional poll-tax on Christians on the ground that they rendered no military service. As to discrimination in other ways, there is evidence that Christians in Persia had to wear distinctive dress by the sixth century.[1] When, therefore, the Arab conquerors took control, things were not very different. Christians, Jews, and Zoroastrians constituted three melets within the population, and though this was a degradation for the Zoroastrians, it left the Christians in much the same condition as before.

In so far as any distinction was made between these melets, the Christians seem to have been the most favoured. Various reasons were advanced to justify their claim to special treatment. It is not certain to what extent these reasons are fact and to what extent fiction, but they may be briefly given: Muhammad was said to have had a Christian teacher, Sergius Bahira; the Patriarch Yeshuyab II (628–643) was said to have seen Muhammad in person, and to have received from him a document conferring special privileges upon Nestorians; the caliph Umar I was asserted to have

[1] Wigram, *History of the Assyrian Church*, p. 230.

confirmed this; and the caliph Ali was said to have given them another letter of protection because they had given his army food at the siege of Mosul. Whether these reasons for favour were sound or not, in all the circumstances the Christians had not a great deal of which to complain, so that a bishop in the province of Adiabene, writing in about 655, soon after the Muslims had taken control, was able to say that the new masters were by no means so bad as they were thought to be, that they were not far removed from Christianity, and that they honoured its clergy and protected its churches.[1]

As to taxation, the caliph Umar I (634–644) had established it on a threefold basis. Muslims had only to pay *zakat*, a kind of poor rate, but non-Muslims had to pay *kharaj*, a tax on land, and also *jizyah*, a poll-tax levied in lieu of military service. But it was soon found that so many converts came over to Islam that it was advisable to distinguish between Arab Muslims and non-Arab Muslims, so non-Arab Muslims were made subject to kharaj. Thus the burden of taxation increased in three grades: Arab Muslims, non-Arab Muslims, non-Muslims. Jizyah was levied in western Persia as early as the time of Umar I, and it is recorded that at the first assessment of non-Muslims in Babylonia 500,000 were found liable. As the tax was a substitute for military service, it was only levied on adult males, monks and the aged being exempted; so the non-Muslim population must have been between one and a half and two millions. It is, however, impossible to

---

[1] Assemani, *Bibliotheca Orientalis*, III. i. 131.

estimate what proportion of these were Christians. The amount of tax was at first one dinar per head, but later this was made a minimum, and those who were better off had to pay more accordingly. (The dinar was a gold coin weighing about 65 grains troy; the British gold sovereign weighs just over 123 grains troy.)

As to other restrictions imposed on the Christians, they had to wear distinctive dress, they were not allowed to ride on horseback, and they were not permitted to carry any weapons; no new churches were to be built on fresh sites, but permission was given to repair or even rebuild existing ones. This last restriction does not appear to have been strictly imposed, as there is evidence that many new churches were built under the Caliphate between the seventh and twelfth centuries.[1] Indeed, the application of all these restrictions was very variable; sometimes they were applied with great exactness, and others added, while at other times they were applied very casually.

During the earlier centuries of Muslim rule the Christians were helped to some extent by the fact that there were more men of education among them than among the Arabs. It thus came about that Christians obtained many official appointments, even at the court of the caliph. The centres of Nestorian culture at Nisibis, Jundishapur, and Merv continued to flourish, and supplied a good proportion of the physicians, teachers, scribes, and accountants, not only for the Caliphate, but for neighbouring parts of Asia. Nor

[1] See Arnold, *The Preaching of Islam*, pp. 58–59.

were Nestorians able to hold only utilitarian positions; they were also esteemed for their general culture. Thus the caliph Abdalmalik (685–705) included among his court poets the Christian Akhtal.

The short reign of Umar (Omar) II (717–720) was one of the periods when Christianity suffered. This was not due to any active repression, but because Umar, in his zeal for Islam, applied many laws which had been disregarded. He decided to return to the earlier taxation methods of his grandfather Umar I, and exempt all Muslims, Arab and non-Arab, from all taxation except zakat. The result was a great increase in professing Muslims, as acceptance of Islam for a non-Arab now meant not only exemption from jizyah, but also from kharaj. This exemption of non-Arab Muslims from kharaj was soon found to cause too drastic a reduction in revenue, and the tax had to be reimposed. But the damage to Christianity had been done, for those who had become Muslims to avoid kharaj could hardly change their faith again on the ground that the tax had been reimposed. Besides, the penalty for renouncing Islam once accepted was death. Umar also enforced the laws of restriction, in particular that against building new churches, and ordered the destruction of all that had been recently built.

The severity of Umar, however, was not continued by his successors. Indeed, under Hisham (724–743) all melets were treated very tolerantly, particularly in the eastern part of the Caliphate (Iraq and Khurasan), which was under the governorship of Khalid. Khalid, whose mother was a Christian, was reputed to be exceptionally considerate to Christians, Jews, and Zoroastrians.

But there was a period of persecution under the caliph Mahdi (775–785). This, as so often, was largely the result of war with the Roman Empire. Although frontier raids had been going on for many years, indeed practically all through the reign of Mansur (754–775), there was no really serious clash until the latter part of Mahdi's reign, from 780 onwards. The concomitant suspicion and persecution of Christians was short and severe. An unpleasant feature of this persecution was cruelty towards Christian women, as many as a thousand lashes with bull's hide thongs being applied to make them apostatize. Nevertheless, in spite of this persecution a new church was built at Baghdad during his reign. It may be noted that Mahdi was even harder on Manichæans[1] and those holding no religion at all.

During the reign of Harun ar-Rashid (785–809) intermittent warfare continued with the Roman Empire, and though there was no definite period of severe persecution like that under Mahdi, the Muslims still regarded the Christians with suspicion, fearing that their sympathies might be with the enemy. Dissatisfied with the conditions of their life under the Caliphate, many Christians emigrated, mostly into the Roman Empire, hoping that there they would be able to

---

[1] Manichæism was a syncretistic religion containing elements drawn from Zoroastrianism, Christianity, and possibly from other faiths also. It was a complete dualism, spiritual and material, good being identified with light and evil with darkness. It was formulated by Mani, who lived in Ctesiphon in the third century A.D., and had a considerable vogue for several centuries in places so far apart as China, India, and the Roman Empire.

practise their faith with fewer disabilities. An additional cause of Christian unhappiness was Harun's impetuosity. He was prone to precipitate action on insufficient evidence, and the Christians suffered for this on several occasions. For instance, one of his officers, Hamdun, told him that in their churches Christians worshipped and bowed down before the bones of the dead. Harun thereupon destroyed several churches, including those at Basrah and Ubullah. It is true that Harun was convinced that he had been misled and had the churches rebuilt, but the incident must have been very disquieting for the Christians none the less. Harun ar-Rashid acted equally precipitately when some monks at Aleppo calumniated the Patriarch of Antioch, destroying many churches in Syria and Palestine. These, of course, were not Nestorian churches, but such an act added to the sense of insecurity felt by all Christians within the Caliphate. But it may be of interest to note that Harun's personal physician was a Nestorian, Gabriel, who is reputed to have been fabulously wealthy.

In the reign of Mamun (813–833) there was a further exodus, due again to wars with the Roman Empire and to the unsettled state of the Caliphate, where internal disorders were beginning to show themselves. A large number of these emigrants settled at Sinope on the coast of the Black Sea. The Emperor Theophilus received them well, and rendered their assimilation easier by enacting that Romans marrying these emigrants should not have their status in any way prejudiced.

During the caliphate of Mutawakkil (846–861) the Christians suffered from a severe application of the repressive laws, but this change for the worse was brought about by the action of one who was himself a Christian. Presumably out of jealousy, a Christian named Ibrahim ben Nuh made complaint to the caliph about the Patriarch Theodosius. The result was that Mutawakkil not only deposed Theodosius (849),[1] but in 850 began to apply the already existing repressive laws with full vigour, and added other disabilities as well. Christians were commanded to wear distinctive garments, 'with a patch on their shirts,'[2] were forbidden to ride on horseback, and were forbidden to attend market on Fridays. The graves of their dead were to be destroyed, their children were not to attend the Muslim schools or be taught Arabic, and a wooden image of the devil was to be nailed to the door of every Christian's house. In addition, a number of churches and monasteries were demolished. Nevertheless, no Christians appear to have been executed for their faith at this time, as Ishudad of Merv, writing about the same period, mentions no recent martyrs. It is again interesting to remark that in spite of these anti-Christian measures, Mutawakkil retained his Christian physicians, a detail which shows that Christians were still ranking high in learned and professional capacities. A few years later, however, there was serious trouble in Homs (Emesa) as a result of these repressive measures.

[1] The chronology here is a little difficult, as the date of Theodosius' accession is generally accepted as 852. Was the dispute over his appointment, resulting in a delay of three years?

[2] *Maris, Amri et Slibæ Commentaria*, edited by Gismondi, fols. 191*a*–191*b*.

In 855 a revolt broke out, in which Christians were joined by Jews, who had been subjected to very similar repressions. The revolt was put down after a vigorous resistance. Many leading Christians and Jews were flogged to death, all churches and synagogues were demolished, and all Christians banished.

After the time of Mutawakkil, the power of the caliphs progressively weakened, and their dominion tended more and more to become dismembered. Egypt became independent under Ahmad ben Tulun in 868, and various other parts of the Caliphate successively gained partial or complete independence. Those who had originally held office as governors began to found minor dynasties, and rendered only a nominal allegiance to the caliph at Baghdad. Thus a situation arose which was internally unstable and outwardly an invitation to aggression. The situation was made worse by the action of the caliphs in endeavouring to strengthen their position by hiring mercenaries from Turkestan. These mercenaries gradually gained influence, and by the tenth century Turkish officers dominated the policy of the caliphs. Their practice was to concede great respect and titular authority to the caliph, but to control all practical affairs themselves. They were not, however, united among themselves, being as prone to faction as the Arabs and Persians whom they had displaced from power. Grave internal unrest therefore continued, and the setting up of minor dynasties in various parts of the Caliphate. Indeed, on several occasions the caliph had little even nominal power outside Baghdad itself.

During such a period it is not surprising that the lot of the Christians was always uncertain and often unhappy. Harassed authorities were hardly likely to be particularly solicitous about the welfare of a melet when the Caliphate itself was in danger, and when trouble arose it was often because the melet restrictions had been laxly applied, advantage of the laxness had been taken by the Christians, and the Muslim populace had taken matters into its own hands. Thus there were several instances of Muslim mob violence against Christians during the caliphate of Muqtadir (908–932). The Muslim populace destroyed several churches in Palestine, including those at Ramleh, Askelon and Cæsarea. These were probably Catholic churches; but at Damascus they destroyed not only the Catholic church of Mart Maryam, but also a Nestorian church. That was in 924. At about the same time there was trouble in Egypt over the collection of jizyah, an attempt being made to collect it from monks and bishops, who were supposed to be exempt.

There was similar trouble in the time of the Patriarch John V (1001–1011). According to the somewhat involved account given by Mari,[1] a Muslim crowd, presumably in Baghdad, suspected that a man who had been found dead was killed by a Christian, a certain Abu Mansur ben al-Daraji. They accordingly attacked the Jacobite church of Mar Thoma, and in the ensuing confusion the church caught fire. The church collapsed, and a great number of people perished. It must be recorded to the credit of the Muslim authorities

[1] Op. cit., fols. 217a–218a.

Gc

that the lawyers decided that the guilt rested on the man who instigated the attack on the church, and that he should be punished. No attack was made at that time on any other church in the locality.

It is possible to make a very interesting comparison between the Christian and Muslim points of view by comparing two statements on these restrictions which cannot differ in date by more than a few years. According to Mari,[1] in the days of the Patriarch John VI (1013–1020), the Christians 'were compelled to wear distinctive dress, and a number deserted the faith on account of the trials, woes, and injuries that befell them. And the people of the western parts were prevented from carrying out their funeral processions by day; and the people of the Third Quarter [in Baghdad], as many as were not religious, became Muslims, and there was great affliction. And part of the woodwork at the rear of the mosque of ar-Rusafat was burnt; and it was laid to the charge of the Christians. But when the government of the caliph al-Qadir learnt the truth of the matter, they prevented the Muslims from carrying out their design of attacking the Christians. . . . And the people suffered trials, and made their prayers by night, and offered the prayers of Ascension Day by night. And the Christians were compelled to wear distinctive dress, and to ride on mules and asses [only], and to dismiss the slaves and maid-servants from their houses.' It is true that such restrictions must have been very irksome, and that at times it cost a great deal in the way of patience and pride to be a Christian.

[1] Op. cit., fols. 220a–220b.

But irksomeness is hardly to be ranked with persecution, and it is significant that while Mari mentions
trials and woes in a general way, the items he par-
ticularizes are not specially or exceptionally grievous –
they are just the expected lot of melets.

Writing at about the same time, Mawardi, a Muslim
lawyer, gives a summary of the melet laws as applied
to the Christians[1]: 'In the poll-tax contract there are
two clauses, one of which is indispensable and the other
commendable. The former includes six articles:
(1) they must not attack nor pervert the sacred book
[i.e. the Koran], (2) nor accuse the Prophet [Mu-
hammad] of falsehood, nor refer to him with contempt,
(3) nor speak of the religion of Islam to blame or con-
travert it, (4) nor approach a Muslim woman with a
view either to illicit relations or to marriage, (5) nor
turn a Muslim from the faith, nor harm him in person
or possessions, (6) nor help the enemies or receive any
of their spies. These are the duties which are strictly
obligatory on them, and to which they must conform.
The second clause, which is only commendable, also
deals with six points: (1) change of external appearance
by wearing a distinctive mark, the *ghiyar*, and the
special waistbelt, *zunnar*, (2) prohibition of erecting
buildings higher than those of the Muslims; they must
only be of equal height or less, (3) prohibition of offend-
ing the ears of Muslims by the sound of the bell, *naqus*,
by reading their books, and by their claims concerning
Uzair [Ezra] and the Messiah, (4) prohibition of

---

[1] Quoted and translated from Mawardi, *Al-ahkam as-sultaniyya*, by
Browne, *Eclipse of Christianity in Asia*, p. 46.

drinking wine publicly and of displaying their crosses and swine, (5) the obligation to proceed secretly to the burial of their dead without a display of tears and lamentations, (6) prohibition of riding on horses, whether pure-bred or mixed, though they are allowed to use mules and asses. These six commendable prescriptions are not necessarily included in the contract of protection, unless they have been expressly stipulated, in which case they are strictly obligatory. The fact of contravening them when they have been stipulated does not entail breach of the contract, but the unbelievers are compelled by force to respect them, and are punished for having violated them. They do not incur punishment when nothing has been stipulated about it.'

Comparison of the statements of Mari and Mawardi suggests that the difference consists more in the point of view than in the actual facts; and while we must by no means minimize the inconveniences and indignities to which Christians under the Caliphate were subject, and the occasional persecutions, it seems clear that their lot, so far as official treatment was concerned, was no worse than it had been under the Sassanids.

2. INTERNAL CONDITION

In spite of the fact that conditions under the Caliphate were not very different from those which had obtained under the Sassanids, the Nestorian Church had no similar record of steady and consistent advance. During the first three centuries of the Caliphate it is

true that there was a considerable increase in the
number of churches, and an increase also in the wealth
and standing of the Christian community. But at the
same time an insidious change was coming over the
character of the Nestorian Christians. They were
becoming more influential in practically all walks of
life than was either good for themselves or pleasing to
the Arabs. This resulted in increased worldliness in
their own outlook and in increased Muslim antipathy
against them. Thus it came about that the advance
during the first three centuries of the Caliphate was
followed by three centuries of almost continuous
decline; and although, as has been seen, the lot of
Christians during the last three centuries was harder
than it had been during the first three, they were
partly themselves to blame. Even so, their subjection,
though irksome, was scarcely comparable to the persecutions under the Sassanids, which had never brought
about permanent weakening of the Persian Church.
So that, though unsettled times and Muslim oppression
undoubtedly contributed something to the decline of
the Persian Nestorian Church during the eleventh to
thirteenth centuries, internal causes must not be
ignored.

These generalizations must now be substantiated.
Perhaps the root of the matter is to be sought in the
growth of the Christians in wealth and power. To see
members of a non-Muslim melet surpassing themselves
both in means and in influence naturally made Muslims
angry and envious; and there is no doubt that though
the Arab was a good warrior, the traditions and habits of

the Nestorians made them superior to the invader in business affairs and in all pursuits where education counted. As to their wealth, the churches which they were able to erect from time to time when restrictions were relaxed are reputed to have been elaborate and expensive buildings; for instance, in 759, during the reign of Mansur (754–775), Cyprian, bishop of Nisibis, built a new church there at a cost of 56,000 dinars (£30,000 gold). Evidence of the wealth of individuals is not easy to obtain, but Gabriel, Nestorian physician to Harun ar-Rashid, is reputed to have had a private fortune equivalent to several million pounds sterling; and the magnitude of the bribes paid by some of the patriarchs, which will be mentioned in more detail a little later, also testifies to the fact that the Nestorians were a wealthy melet: the patriarch of a poor church cannot pay bribes running into the equivalent of hundreds and, in at least two cases, thousands of pounds. Now wealth, though not evil in itself, often has two unfortunate results: the engendering of a materialistic outlook in the possessor, and the arousing of envy in the beholder. It is hardly to be expected that the Nestorians were altogether free from the former defect, any more than that the Muslims were free from the latter.

Position may arouse envy just as easily as wealth, and it was a long time before Arab physicians were able to displace the Nestorians. The physicians at the court of the caliph were usually Nestorians until about the eleventh century. In 765 the caliph Mansur summoned Georgius from the Nestorian medical school at Jundishapur to be court physician at his new capital, Baghdad. From that time forward Christian physicians were held in high esteem, and even persecuting caliphs retained their Christian doctors, as has been mentioned in the cases of Harun ar-Rashid and Mutawakkil. The court physicians, together with Christian scribes, secretaries, and other similar officials, constituted quite an important group in the caliph's entourage, and orthodox Muslims not seldom felt that there was too much Christian influence in State affairs.

It was particularly offensive to many Muslims when, as sometimes happened, a Christian was given a position of direct authority. They might recognize the value of Christians as secretaries and doctors, but they resented a Christian having administrative power over them. A notable example was the appointment by the caliph Mutadid (892–902) of a Christian to the governorship of Anbar, an important town on the Euphrates about forty-two miles from Baghdad. Envy at such appointments naturally caused some Muslims to consider that the laws of restriction were too leniently applied. This outlook is reflected in the writings of Abu Uthman Amr ben Bahr al-Jahiz, who died in 869. He refers to the wealth of many of the Christians, to their use of horses, and to their ignoring other restrictions. As to distinctive dress, he complains that the special waist-belt was often worn under other clothes, and so out of sight, and that some had given up wearing it altogether. He says that payment of jizyah was often avoided, even by those well able to pay. Indeed, in many ways it would appear that

Christians claimed much the same status as their Muslim overlords, and it would seem that 'the blood of the Catholicus and the Metropolitan and the Bishop was worth as much as the blood of Jafar and Ali and al-Abas and Hamza.'[1]

Another unfortunate result of the prosperity of the Nestorians during the earlier centuries of the Caliphate was that the position of the patriarch became one of considerable worldly importance, and the office was sought by some whose interests were political and social rather than spiritual. The patriarch came to be closely associated with the court circle, partly owing to the fact that his seat had been removed from Seleucia-Ctesiphon to Baghdad. This change took place about 775, and was due to the fact that Seleucia-Ctesiphon was ceasing to be a place of any importance, while Baghdad had become the capital of the Caliphate. The Arabs had wrought great havoc at Seleucia and Ctesiphon at the time of their invasion, and the two cities never fully recovered. What was left of them was named by the Arabs 'al-Madaïn' (the (two) cities), and though Madaïn continued to exist, it retained only the shadow of its former greatness. When, therefore, the second Abbasid caliph, Mansur, wished to have a strong capital city in Mesopotamia, he considered it wiser to start afresh rather than to revive Ctesiphon. He accordingly chose a site on the Tigris about fifteen miles above Ctesiphon, and built there a strong citadel. The plan adopted was circular, with a mosque and his own palace in the centre. The outer wall was

[1] Quoted by Browne, op. cit., p. 48, from J. Finkel, *Three Essays*, p. 18.

over three miles round, and had gates toward the four
cardinal points. The city soon grew beyond the
confines of this original plan, and, during the middle
ages, Baghdad came to rank as one of the leading cities
of the world. The city was begun in 762 and completed
by 766. Within ten years of its completion the Patriarch of the East had made it his seat, the change
taking place in the patriarchate of Hananyeshu II
(774–779). In spite of this change, the title Patriarch
of Seleucia-Ctesiphon still continued to be used.

From that time the association between patriarch
and caliph was often a close one, and as civil and
religious head of a wealthy melet, the office of Nestorian
Patriarch was of considerable importance. As a
result, there was sometimes considerable competition
for the position, and it reflects rather unfavourably on
the general tone of the Nestorian Church at this period
that such competition occasionally took an unseemly
form, with a consequent ill effect on the serenity of the
hierarchy. A notable example was the election of the
Patriarch Timothy I (779–823).[1] His election was
largely assured by leading the electors to imagine that
some sacks, presumably full of money, would be the
reward of his supporters. After he was duly elected,
it was found that the sacks contained only stones, and
those who expressed a very natural indignation were
blandly told that 'The priesthood is not sold for
money.' Nor was Timothy without imitators in using
real or pretended bribery. Thus in 912 the Patriarch

---

[1] Following, as to this date, the *Encyclopædia Britannica*, xxi. 724. For
other opinions see p. 138.

Abraham III spent 30,000 dinars in intrigues against the Orthodox Church; in 1148 the Patriarch Yeshuyab V secured his election by a bribe of 5,000 dinars; and a century later at least two other patriarchs secured election in a similar manner.

The Nestorian Patriarch was not only head of the Nestorian Church, but from about the middle of the eleventh century he was given civil jurisdiction over Christians of all kinds in the Caliphate. Thus in a diploma of appointment dating from the early thirteenth century we read: 'The Sublime Authority empowers thee to be installed at Baghdad as Catholicus of the Nestorians, as also for the other Christians in Muslim lands, as representative in these lands of the Rum, Jacobites, and Melkites.'[1]

Although the office of patriarch was such an important one, there were vacancies lasting several years at various times during the Caliphate. Le Quien[2]

---

[1] Up till the eleventh century the term Melkite was used by Easterns to describe all Christians either actually in the Church of the Roman Empire or in agreement with that Church. The word is derived from the common Semitic root for 'king,' the triliteral root *mlk*, which appears in Hebrew as *melek*, in Aramaic as *melak*, in Syriac as *malka*, and in Arabic as *malik*. The word Melkite thus really means 'king's men,' i.e. those in religious agreement with the Roman Emperor. After the Great Schism had divided the original Catholic Church into Roman Catholic and Greek Orthodox, a division which may be reckoned as complete by 1054, the word is often used in reference to both Catholic and Orthodox, and sometimes for Uniates (see the note on p. 109). The use of the word Rum is a little uncertain. It may refer to the Roman Empire, in which case after 1054 ecclesiastically it would imply the Greek Orthodox Church; or it may refer to the city of Rome, in which case after 1054 ecclesiastically it would imply the Roman Catholic Church. As used here it probably means the latter, for we know that for a time during the Middle Ages there was a Roman Catholic Church at Baghdad. In this quotation Rum and Melkite may therefore be taken to refer to Roman Catholic and Greek Orthodox respectively.

[2] *Oriens Christianus*, ii. 1121–1140.

supplies a list of the dates: 681–686, 698–714, 726–728 (or 728–730), 849–852, 872–877, 986–987, 1038–1041, and three short vacancies of two to three years each about 1094, 1132, and 1136. These vacancies were not always due to external influences or Muslim hostility, but sometimes arose as a result of the unpleasant competition which was so liable to accompany the election of a new patriarch, as was instanced in the case of Timothy. When such competition became too acute the see would remain vacant until the contending parties reached agreement or compromise, often a matter of years. The reason must have been internal in the first and third periods in Le Quien's list, as these dates fall in the caliphates of Abdalmalik and Hisham respectively, both of whom were tolerant toward Christianity. The vacancy from 849 to 852 was due to the action of the caliph Mutawakkil, but it is not probable that he would have taken the action he did if the Christians had kept their dispute to themselves (see p. 95).

We are thus driven to the conclusion that the decline of the Nestorian Church during the latter centuries of the Caliphate was to some extent due to defects in the Nestorian community itself. These defects may be summarized as an increasingly material outlook due to prosperity and influence, and a loosening grip on the essentials of their faith. As Browne remarks, it is not permissible to explain the decline as solely due to Muslim persecution, for far worse persecutions had failed to stop the growth of the Church in the time of the Sassanids. 'One is therefore bound to conclude that the failure of the Christian community to hold its own, and increase in numbers, must have been due to the feebleness of their Christian faith.'[1]   Not only so, but, as has been seen, the persecutions were sometimes partly brought about by their own indiscretion.   Even Assemani, himself a Syrian, writes: 'Not rarely the tempest of persecution was aroused by the mutual jealousy of the Christians themselves, the licence of the priests, the arrogance of the leaders, the tyrannical power of the magnates, and especially the altercations of the physicians and scribes about the highest authority over their people.'[2]

Nevertheless, it must not be forgotten that there were three centuries of advance before this downward tendency began to operate, and during those three centuries there was considerable extension of the Nestorian Church both within and beyond the Caliphate.   Eminent among those who rendered effective service to the Church during this period of advance was the Patriarch Timothy I, who held office for the exceptional term of over forty years (779–823).   That Timothy was not irreproachable has already been seen with regard to the mode of his election, an incident which caused him some little trouble for several years afterwards.   Some wished to displace him, and to set up Ephraim of Jundishapur in his stead.   However, he eventually stilled the opposition and set about the serious work of his office; and whatever doubts we may

[1] Op. cit., p. 63.

[2] *Bibliotheca Orientalis*, III. ii. 100.   The last sentence is a reference to the disputes which so often arose over the election of patriarchs.

have as to the spirituality of his character, he was without question an efficient administrator and skilful in dealing with doctrinal matters.

He did what he could to conciliate other sects such as the Maronites,[1] who were monothelites, in order to unify the Christian Church in Persia. But when conciliation was rejected, or was obviously impossible, he was a strenuous opponent, as for instance against Catholics, who at this time had a bishop at Baghdad, Jacobites, Henanians, and Masalians.[2] As patriarch he kept a firm control over his patriarchate, checking the pretensions of some of the more ambitious metropolitans. He put down certain abuses, and imposed celibacy on bishops and monks. The ordinary clergy, however, were still allowed to marry. He was alive to the importance of education, and wrote thus to a newly appointed bishop: 'Take care of the schools with all your heart. Remember that the school is the mother and nurse of sons of the church.'[3] He got on well with the caliphs, and won the gratitude of Harun ar-Rashid and his wife Zubaidah by a clever solution to a difficult problem of divorce and re-marriage. The

[1] The Maronites were a sect of obscure origin, mostly to be found in the Lebanon district. They may have originated with Yuhanna Marun (*ob.* 707), and were certainly believers in monothelitism (that Christ had only one will, the divine), from the eighth century onwards. Since 1445 they have been Uniates. (A Uniate Church is an Eastern Church retaining its own rite and hierarchy, but acknowledging the supremacy of the Pope and accepting Roman Catholic dogma.)

[2] The Masalians were a small sect which flourished to some extent in Syria and Mesopotamia from about the sixth till the twelfth century. They were fairly strong in Adiabene and just south of Nisibis. They denied all sacraments and forms of hierarchy, and admitted no means of grace but prayer.

[3] Fortescue, *Lesser Eastern Churches*, p. 95.

details are obscure, but the whole transaction seems to
have borne testimony more to Timothy's worldly
wisdom than to his spirituality.[1]   Another example of
his sagacity and readiness is afforded by his skilful
reply to an awkward question which Harun put to
him: 'O father of the Christians, tell me briefly which
religion is the true one in God's eyes.'   Timothy in-
stantly answered: 'That religion of which the rules and
precepts correspond with the works of God.'   The
answer neither belies Christianity nor offends Islam;
and it must be remembered that though Christians
were tolerated, any slight from them upon Muhammad
or Islam would be very seriously regarded (see p. 99).

As to organization and administration, the Nestorian
Church probably reached its most efficient condition
during this period.   The power of the patriarch was
jealously guarded, and apart altogether from his
ecclesiastical authority, his status as head of the melet
must have increased his power considerably.   Although the general method of administration remained
unaltered, the system was worked more consistently.
Thus the principle of grouping the churches into
metropolitan provinces was more thoroughly applied,
and by the tenth century, instead of the seven metropolitans under Babai in 497, there were at least twenty.
The number of bishops without a metropolitan over
them was also greatly reduced, the tendency being to
bring all bishoprics into metropolitan provinces.

The growth of the Church during the eighth, ninth,

---

[1] The details are in Labourt, *De Timotheo I Nestorianorum Patriarcha et
Christianorum condicione sub Caliphis*, p. 35.

and tenth centuries and its decline during the eleventh, twelfth, and thirteenth, were gradual processes; it is particularly important to notice that the decline was progressive and not sudden. It has sometimes been supposed that the grave declension of the Nestorian Church was due altogether to the Mongols. This is not so; and although the Mongols wrought considerable havoc in certain areas (see pp. 143–144), and perhaps gave the *coup de grâce* to many already waning churches, the decline was evident long before they invaded the Caliphate. Nevertheless, there is no doubt that many churches came to their end as a result of the great disturbance which the Mongol expansion caused in Central Asia and the Caliphate during the twelfth to fourteenth centuries. When we know that a certain town was sacked and practically destroyed by the Mongols in a certain year, and when the last reference to the church in that place is within the century prior to that date, we may often safely conclude that church and town perished together; for the date of the last reference to a church does not necessarily coincide with the actual end of that church. When we say that a church was last heard of or mentioned at a certain date, it may often well be that the church continued for quite a long time after that. The general impression is therefore one of steady decline, accelerated by the troubled internal state of the Caliphate during its later years, and in some districts culminating in final extinction by Mongol invasions of the early thirteenth century.

All this can be most clearly shown by following the

fortunes of the patriarchate province by province, and indicating the establishing of churches during the former three centuries of the Caliphate and their disappearance during the latter three. It is naturally not to be expected that all churches and provinces would rise and fall together, but on the average the middle of the tenth century seems to have been the time of greatest extent of the Nestorian Church in the Caliphate.

In the Caliphate itself there were fifteen metropolitan provinces,[1] instead of the seven under Babai. The additional provinces did not all represent advance into new areas, many of them being former bishoprics which had been elevated into metropolitan sees, in some cases owing to actual administrative need and in others *jure dignitatis*.

Provinces in the Caliphate:

(1) *Province of Patriarchalis*.

In this province three new bishoprics were established in the eighth century, Tirhana, Kosra, and Buazicha[2]; two in the ninth, Ocbara and Wasit; and two in the tenth, Radan and Naphara. During the same period a few new schools were founded, including one at Tirhana about 730 and one at Mahuza, a suburb of Baghdad, in 832. But in the eleventh century four bishoprics became extinct, those of Hira, Sena, Radan, and Buazicha, and in the twelfth five more, Anbar, Naphara, Kosra, Badraia, and Naamania. This left

---

[1] The exact number of metropolitan provinces is not quite certain, as the two most ancient authorities, the *Notitia* of Elias Damascenus (ninth century) and the *Tabula* of Amrus (fourteenth century), do not agree. The reservations made on p. 56 must therefore apply here also.

[2] Not the same place as Buazicha in Garamæa, p. 115.

only four: the metropolitan at Kaskar, and bishops at Tirhana, Ocbara, and Wasit. Of these, only the bishopric at Tirhana outlasted the Caliphate, the metropolitan see itself becoming extinct in 1222, Ocbara in 1224, and Wasit at about the same time. One solitary event relieves the continuity of the decline: the restoration by the patriarch Elias III of the monastery of Dorkena, which had evidently been allowed to fall into decay. This was in 1180.

(2) *Province of Jundishapur.*

In this province a school was founded at Lapeta[1] in 834. It was subsequently transferred to Jundishapur. The bishopric of Ahwaz became extinct in the ninth century, and that at Suster probably just before the end of this period.

(3) *Province of Nisibis.*

In this province considerable advance was made, and comparatively little of the ground gained was lost. It is to be noted that this province, together with the provinces of Mosul and Atropatene, which cover the only area where the Nestorian Church afterwards survived, was becoming a strong centre of Nestorian Christianity long before the end of the Caliphate; so that it is hardly accurate to think of the remnant 'fleeing to the hill country of Kurdistan and establishing themselves there' at the time of the Mongol expansion or at the time of Timur i Leng: the area was

[1] Unless Lapeta is merely a variant of Beth Lapat, the old Syriac name for Jundishapur. In that case the school was at Jundishapur all the time.

Hc

becoming a Nestorian stronghold long before that. Naturally, when those invasions did take place, many Nestorian refugees made their way to Kurdistan from other parts, because it was further from the storm centre than regions further south and east, and because they knew they would be among their co-religionists; but they did not have to establish churches, for they were already there. Thus while at the beginning of this period we only know of the metropolitan at Nisibis and bishops at Bakerda, Balada, and Arzun, together with the bishopric of Maiperkat, which was probably by this time reckoned in this province, by the end of the period not only were all these still in existence, but additional bishoprics had become established at Gezluna, Mardis, and Amida (modern Diarbekr). During the same period only two bishoprics had been established and since lapsed, Harran and Raqqa, a record which compares very favourably with that of other provinces.

(4) *Province of Teredon.*

This province continued uneventfully until about the end of this period, the metropolitan see itself (Basrah) being last heard of in 1222, and the bishopric of Deste-sana in 1260, just after this period. There was also for a time a church at Ubullah.

(5) *Province of Mosul.*

This, as already mentioned, was one of the regions of advance. It became a province in 651, with the seat of the metropolitan at Mosul. The bishopric of

Nineveh, already in existence, was taken into this province, and other bishoprics were established at about the following dates: Beth-Bagas, 686; Haditha, 714; Dasena, 754; Nuhadra, 963; Ormia (modern Urmi), 1068. All these bishoprics, together with those of Mosul and Nineveh, survived this period.

(6) *Province of Adiabene.*

Metropolitans continued at Erbil and bishops at Maalta throughout this period, but the bishopric of Honita seems to have disappeared early in the ninth century, and that at Zuabia by the end of the twelfth. There was also a bishopric at Castom from about the end of the tenth till about the middle of the twelfth century.

(7) *Province of Garamæa.*

Metropolitans continued at Karkha and bishops at Dakuka throughout the period. The bishopric of Sciaarchadata had become extinct in the sixth century, and that at Marangerd in the seventh, but a bishopric was established at Buazicha,[1] probably in the tenth century, which continued for the remainder of this period. There were bishoprics at Arzuna for a time during the seventh century, at Tahal and Telach during the eighth and ninth, and at Chanigiara for a time during the ninth century.

(8) *Province of Halwan.*

This was a new province, established with a metropolitan at Halwan in 754. A bishopric was established

[1] Not the same place as Buazicha in Babylonia, p. 112.

at Hamadan toward the end of the tenth century. Neither is heard of after the end of the twelfth century.

(9) *Province of Fars.*

Although for a time evidently a very important one, our information about this province is scanty. The only churches definitely known to have existed in this area at the time of Babai were those at Rawardshir and Drangerda, but there is no trace of the latter after the sixth century. It is uncertain when there were first metropolitans for Fars: possibly toward the end of the sixth century. Their seat is also uncertain, but was probably Rawardshir. The Province included many widely scattered islands, and there were bishops on the islands of Dirin, Ormuz, Socotra (the ancient Dioscoris), Catara and Masamig (small islands near Socotra), and bishops or churches at Shiraz, Shapur, and Astachar. All dates are uncertain, though the most flourishing period seems to have been about the seventh to ninth centuries. All except the bishopric of the island of Socotra had become extinct some time before the end of this period.

This province seems to have caused Seleucia-Ctesiphon a certain amount of anxiety, for the Patriarch Yeshuyab III (650–660) had to write reproving the metropolitan for neglecting his duties, not only in Fars but also in other places under his care, notably India. There was trouble again in the time of the Patriarch Timothy I (779–823). According to Barhebræus,[1] a Jacobite, the metropolitan and bishops of Fars declared

---

[1] Quoted by Assemani, *Bibliotheca Orientalis*, III. ii. 422.

themselves independent of Timothy and Seleucia-Ctesiphon, claiming to be Thomas Christians. Barhebræus quotes them as saying: 'Nos Thomæ Apostoli discipuli sumus, et nihil nobis cum sede Maris commune est.' "The seat of Maris' is, of course, Seleucia-Ctesiphon, Maris (Mares, Mari) being the legendary founder of many Persian churches. He was supposed to have been a disciple of Addai of Edessa, who had been one of the seventy, and to have appointed Papa Bar Aggai (*floruit* 315) as first bishop of Seleucia-Ctesiphon. (The chronology implied is quite impossible.) The metropolitan of Fars had hitherto held jurisdiction over India also, but after this incident Timothy appointed a separate metropolitan for India. As to the threatened secession, nothing more seems to have come of it. It may have been merely a spirited protest against the sterner patriarchal discipline imposed by Timothy, to which reference has already been made (p. 109).

(10) *Province of Khurasan.*

We only know of metropolitans of Merv and bishops of Nishapur, the last metropolitan definitely mentioned being in 1070. But it may safely be assumed that the Nestorian Church in this province was destroyed at the same time as the cities of Merv and Nishapur, which received terrible treatment at the hands of Tule, son of Jenghiz Khan, in 1221 (see p. 143).

(11) *Province of Atropatene.*

This was the third of the regions where permanent advance was made. Metropolitans continued at

Taurisium all through the period, and bishoprics were established at Maragha and Achlat in the eighth century, both of which continued into the next period. Although there was thus a net advance, it must be recorded that for a short time at the beginning of the thirteenth century there were bishoprics at Cadhira, Hesna, and Salmas. These did not survive.

(12) *Province of Herat.*

The bishopric of Herat became a metropolitan see probably in the eighth century, and the bishopric of Segestan may have been associated with it. Both became extinct about the eleventh century; or possibly they shared the fate of the churches of Merv and Nishapur under Tule, in which case we should date their extinction 1221.

(13) *Province of Arran.*

There were metropolitans at Bardaa from about 900 to 1200.

(14) *Province of Rai.*

The bishopric of Rai became a metropolitan see about 778, and the bishopric of Ispahan was possibly associated with it. Both became extinct by about the end of the twelfth century, and in these cases also Tule may have been responsible.

(15) *Province of Dailam.*

There were metropolitans for this province at Mukar from about 780 till 1000. The first was sent by the Patriarch Timothy, and was murdered by the

Dailamites. The work of the province was very difficult throughout its existence.

These fifteen provinces covered the area of the old Persian Empire. In addition to the bishoprics which are listed above according to their metropolitan provinces, there are some which we cannot with certainty assign to any particular province, though at this period they were probably linked up with some metropolitan. What little information we have about such places bears out the same general conclusion: a rise followed by a decline. For the sake of completeness a list of them is appended in the approximate order of their origin: Saharzur, Salach, Rhesen, Cadne, Nahz, Dir, Nil, Comar, Sarchesa, Themanon, Berbera, Rostaca. All these bishoprics came into existence during or after the seventh century, and all had disappeared by the end of this period, or very soon afterwards.

To complete the list of Nestorian metropolitan provinces we have only to add the names of the several provinces to which the Nestorian churches in other regions were assigned. They were:

(16) Province of India, with metropolitans, intermittently and at various places, from about 800 till well beyond this period.

(17) Province of China, with metropolitans at Sianfu from about 636 till beyond this period.

(18) Province of Turkestan, with metropolitans at Samarqand from about 781 till probably the end of the twelfth century or the time of Tule.

(19) Province of Damascus, with metropolitans to
     care for Nestorians in the West generally, from
     632[1] till the end of the twelfth century.
(20) Province of Jerusalem, with metropolitans to
     care for Nestorian pilgrims and any other
     Palestinian Nestorians. Ranked as bishops
     from 895, but as metropolitans from 1065.
     Extinct by about 1616.

These are given here in order to give a complete
list of the Nestorian metropolitan provinces at the time
of the Nestorian Church's greatest strength and extent.
Details will be given under the appropriate geographical headings (pp. 125–135). Some writers give
a longer list of metropolitans,[2] including metropolitans
for other parts of China and Turkestan, and even for
Tibet and Java. The evidence is often insecure, and
if such were ever appointed, the status was often merely
titular.

As the tenth century was the time of the greatest
extent of the Nestorian Church in Persia, it may be
desirable to set out a list of the metropolitan provinces
existing at that time, together with their known dependent bishoprics. A comparison with the list given
on p. 57 will show how greatly the Church had
grown, particularly in the provinces of Patriarchalis,
Mosul and Nisibis; and the list will also make clear the
extent of the decline between the tenth and thirteenth

[1] But see pp. 125–126.
[2] Assemani gives twenty-five, op. cit., III. ii. 630, and Stewart, *Nestorian
Missionary Enterprise*, reckons as many as thirty-two, according to his
map.

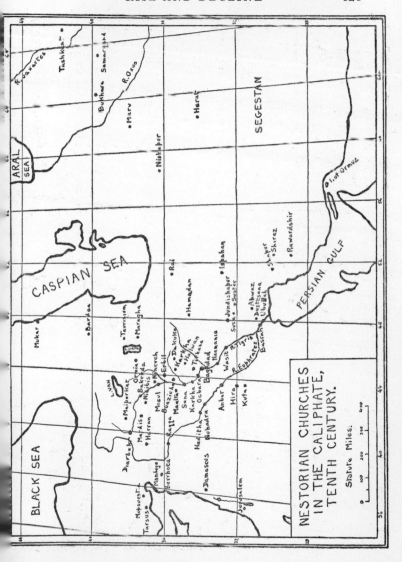

NESTORIAN CHURCHES
IN THE CALIPHATE,
TENTH CENTURY.

Statute Miles:
0 100 200 300 400

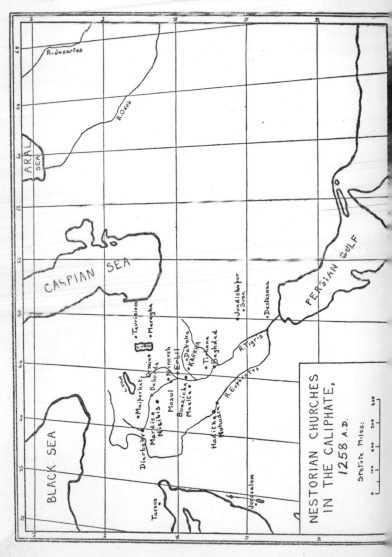

NESTORIAN CHURCHES IN THE CALIPHATE, 1258 A.D.

centuries, for only the places printed in heavier type are known to have still possessed bishops or churches when Hulagu captured Baghdad in 1258.

The Nestorian Church in Persia, A.D. 1000: Seat of the Patriarch: Baghdad.

(1) Province of Patriarchalis. Metropolitan at Kaskar, bishops at Hira, Anbar, Karkha,[1] Naamania, Sena, Buazicha,[1] Badraia, Tirhana, Kosra, Ocbara, Wasit, Radan, Naphara.

(2) Province of Jundishapur. Metropolitan at Jundishapur, bishops at Susa, Ahwaz, Suster.

(3) Province of Nisibis. Metropolitan of Nisibis, bishops at Bakerda, Balada, Arzun, Gesluna, Mardis, Amida (modern Diarbekr), Maiperkat, Harran, Raqqa.

(4) Province of Teredon. Metropolitan of Basrah, bishops at Ubullah, Destesana, Nahar al-Marah.

(5) Province of Mosul. Metropolitan at Mosul, bishops at Nineveh, Beth-Bagas, Haditha, Dasena, Nuhadra, Ormia (modern Urmi).

(6) Province of Adiabene. Metropolitan at Erbil, bishops at Maalta, Zuabia, Caftoun.

(7) Province of Garamæa. Metropolitan at Karkha,[2] bishops at Dakuka and Buazicha.[2]

(8) Province of Halwan. Metropolitan at Halwan, bishop at Hamadan.

[1] These two places are to be distinguished from those bearing the same names in the province of Garamæa.
[2] These two places are to be distinguished from those bearing the same names in the province of Patriarchalis.

(9) Province of Fars. Metropolitan at Rawardshir, bishops at Shiraz, Shapur and Astachar, and on the islands of **Socotra**, Catara, Masamig, **Dirin** and **Ormuz**.

(10) Province of Khurasan. Metropolitan at Merv, bishop at Nishapur.

(11) Province of Atropatene. Metropolitan at **Taurisium**, bishops at **Maragha** and **Achlat**.

(12) Province of Herat. Metropolitan at Herat, a bishop for Segestan.

(13) Province of Arran. Metropolitan at Bardaa.

(14) Province of Rai. Metropolitan at Rai, a bishop at Ispahan.

(15) Province of Dailam. Metropolitan at Mukar.

The maps on pp. 121 and 122 respectively show the difference between the Nestorian Church in Persia and the areas immediately adjoining in the tenth century and in the year 1258. It is noticeable that the greatest decline took place in the eastern and southern parts of the Caliphate, and that the centre of the Church's strength moved from the region around Baghdad to the regions around and to the north of Mosul.

3. NESTORIAN CHURCHES OUTSIDE PERSIA

(i) *Arabia.*

There is very little definite information about Christianity in Arabia after the middle of the seventh century, and such information as we have consists of a few isolated references: a Nestorian synod was held in southern Arabia in 676, presided over by the Patriarch Georgius (660–680)[1]; the Patriarch Timothy I appointed a bishop for Sana (Yaman) at the end of the eighth century; in 991 the Patriarch John IV wrote a letter to a priest in Yaman answering certain questions. There are occasional references to bishops of Najran; but as the caliph Umar I had deported all Najranites who refused to embrace Islam to Kufa in Iraq, it seems probable that references as late as 864 and 935 to bishops of Najran refer to the Najran community at Kufa. Christianity also lingered on in a few of the nomad tribes, such as the Banu Salih, for as late as 779 we hear of the caliph Mahdi trying to compel them to become Muslims, and they again suffered under the caliph Mamun in 823. But it is fairly safe to assume that by the end of the tenth century Christianity in Arabia was virtually extinct, until European missionaries began work there towards the end of the nineteenth century.

(ii) *The West.*

The extension of the power of the Caliphate over regions which had formerly been under the Roman Empire made it possible for Nestorian missions to be sent where previously the Roman authorities would have forbidden them. Thus after 636, by which time the Muslims had conquered Palestine and Syria, Nestorian churches began to appear in those regions, and a little later in Cilicia, Cyprus, and even Egypt, the stronghold of monophysitism. According to

[1] Mingana, *Bulletin of the John Rylands Library*, x. 2. 439.

Wiltsch,[1] the first metropolitan of Damascus was appointed in 632. This seems a little early, but we may safely assume that a Nestorian metropolitan was there before the end of the seventh century. Under his care were many presumably small Nestorian congregations, for though such communities are named as existing at Mambeg, Mopsuestia and elsewhere, the only bishops mentioned are one for Egypt, in the middle of the eighth century, one for Berrhoea, in the middle of the eleventh, and one for Tarsus a little later. These western Nestorian churches do not seem to have made much headway, and gradually died out. By the end of the twelfth century only the bishopric of Tarsus remained, which lasted till the middle of the fifteenth century.

The Nestorians also had a bishop at Jerusalem, but he was there more for the sake of pilgrims than for permanent residents. It was also probably felt by the Nestorians that, like the rest of Christendom, they ought to have a representative there; a bishop was therefore appointed in 893. After 1065 the bishops of Jerusalem were ranked as metropolitans. They are not heard of after 1616.

(iii) *India.*

In this period the first reference to the Church in India, though an oblique and tenuous one, is nevertheless interesting enough to be cited. In 883 King Alfred of England sent Sighelm, bishop of Shireburn, and a priest, Athelstan, to India with votive offerings for

---

[1] *Geography and Statistics of the Church*, i. 491.

St. Thomas, which he had promised for his successes against the Danes. They presented their offerings, and returned with gifts of jewels and spices.[1]

Didacus de Couto[2] testifies to the existence of Christians in India at about the same time, and says they were to be found at Diamper, Cortale, Cartute, in the kingdom of Malea, at Turubuli, Maota, Batimena, Porea, Travancore, Pimenta, Tetan, Para, and some other places. Metropolitans for India were first appointed in the time of the Patriarch Timothy I (778–823), before which time the Indian churches were under the metropolitan of Fars (see p. 116). Le Quien names a few metropolitans of India from 880. They resided at first in Malabar. The succession shortly became broken, and the Church sent to Baghdad for a new metropolitan. One was sent, and resided at Cranganora, but if he had any successors we know nothing of them. A century or two later Le Quien finds mention of a metropolitan at Patna, in about 1122. Little more is known of the Church in India till the time of Marco Polo (p. 161).

(iv) *Turkestan.*

Central Asia during the Middle Ages was a region of great racial fluidity, and the history of the tribes which successively overflowed from it is not easy to disentangle. They were of nomad habit, and it is not possible to assign a given area to a certain tribe for any great length of time. Their expansive force made

[1] Robinson, *History of Christian Missions*, p. 65, and Fortescue, *Lesser Eastern Churches*, p. 361.
[2] Quoted by Le Quien, *Oriens Christianus*, ii. 1273–1276.

itself felt as far afield as China, India, and eastern Europe, and even if for convenience we classify all these tribes as Tartars[1] and Mongols, their subdivisions and ramifications are almost endless. Nevertheless, there were effective Nestorian missions among them, although from the nature of the case not much reliable detail is available.

In the earlier part of this period, mission work in Turkestan owed much to the administrative ability of the Patriarch Timothy I (pp. 108–110). He was much concerned about the welfare of Nestorian churches in distant parts, and never failed to send help when it was needed or to respond to invitations to open up new areas. Thus he sent many missionaries into Turkestan, some on his own initiative, and some at the request of the heads of certain of the tribes. He appointed a metropolitan for Turkestan, whose seat was at Samarqand, and there were bishops at Bukhara and Tashkent. Few details are known of these missions beyond the fact of their existence. Timothy sent out nearly one hundred missionaries, some of whom were monks and others of whom he ordained as bishops, so that ordinations might be effected and a proper hierarchy established in regions where their work was successful. Of these the names of very few are known, but Shabhalisho is reputed to have been particularly valuable on account of his linguistic abilities. But the fact that a knowledge of Christianity was so widely diffused among the Tartars and Mongols shows that the extent and effectiveness of their work must not be underestimated.

[1] More correctly *Tatar*.

Much of the evidence has been collected by Mingana.[1]

A few centuries later there is evidence of Nestorian activity in Turkestan, particularly further to the north-east, toward Lake Baikal. Though there is again neither the detail nor the certainty we might desire, it seems sufficiently sure, that during the tenth and eleventh centuries several Tartar tribes were entirely or to a great extent Christian, notably the Keraits, Uighurs, Naimans and Merkites. The Kerait capital at this time was Karakoram, where Marco Polo said he found a church. The historical basis of the Prester John legend may well have been a Christian ruler of the Keraits. Some would identify him with one or other of the Unk Khans. This was a hereditary title, and among its forms are Unc Khan and Owang Khan. As Fortescue points out,[2] Owang is not unlike Ioannes, so perhaps the historicity of Prester John is not so dubious as was at one time supposed. Though not Priest and King of a mighty Central Asian empire, he may at least have been Christian ruler of a considerable Tartar tribe. But in any case it is to be doubted whether he would have been powerful enough to lead overwhelming forces to the help of the Crusaders, as in the twelfth century they fondly hoped.

Christianity was therefore widely diffused throughout Turkestan by the twelfth century, and this fact is of considerable importance in relation to the Mongol expansion. It is true that the Mongol expansion under Jenghiz Khan almost obliterated Christianity from

[1] *Bulletin of the John Rylands Library*, ix. 306–308.
[2] *Lesser Eastern Churches*, p. 105.

Western Turkestan and the eastern half of the Caliphate, but that was simply due to the Mongols' terrible methods of warfare, not to any special antipathy to Christianity, as will be made clear in the next chapter. The result, however, was much the same, and the churches at Samarqand, Bukhara, and Tashkent all came to an end when those cities were sacked by the Mongols under Jenghiz Khan and his son Tule just after the beginning of the thirteenth century. But the Nestorian Christian missions in Eastern Turkestan and Mongolia had not been fruitless, and, incongruous though it may seem, there was a considerable Christian element in the armies of Jenghiz Khan; it is recorded that wheeled chapels often accompanied the Mongol hosts. It thus came about that after the terrible upheaval of the latter part of the twelfth and early part of the thirteenth century, there was a period of comparative calm during which Christianity again flourished in Turkestan. What little is known of that revival will be set out in the next chapter (pp. 164–167).

(v) *China.*

The first effective Christian mission to China of which we have any definite knowledge was that sent by the Patriarch Yeshuyab II in about the year 635. Much of our information about Christianity in China during the seventh and eighth centuries is derived from the Nestorian stone of Sianfu. It will be assumed that this stone is to be accepted as trustworthy, though it must be stated that doubts as to its genuineness have

been advanced many times [1] But as what little other
information we have fits in as well as can reasonably
be expected with the statements on this stone, there
seems no great need to question it. The stone was
discovered at Sianfu in 1625, either by Jesuit missionaries or by Chinese who gave them early access to it.
It is nine feet high and three feet wide, and bears a long
inscription in Chinese and Syriac.

According to the inscription, it would appear that
Christianity was brought to China about the year 635
by Alopen,[2] who, coming from Syria with sacred books,
'braved difficulties and dangers.' This was in the time
of the Emperor Tai-tsung (627–650) of the Tang
dynasty. The emperor was favourable to the new
religion, and in 638 issued the following decree:
'Alopen, a Persian monk, bringing the religion of the
Scriptures from far, has come to offer it at the chief
metropolis. The meaning of his religion has been
carefully examined. It is mysterious, wonderful, calm.
It fixes the essentials of life and perfection. It is right
that it should spread through the Empire. Therefore
let the ministers build a monastery in the Ining-fang (a
city square in Sianfu), and let twenty-one men be
admitted as monks.' Alopen was thus able to establish a monastery, and before the end of the century
the new religion had spread through ten provinces,
many more monasteries being founded.

[1] References to a variety of opinions on this stone may be found in
Stewart, *Nestorian Missionary Enterprise*, pp. 170–182.
[2] For variants of this name see the supplemental index, p. 223.
Several writers have suggested that it is simply a corrupted form of the
Syriac *rabban*, monk.

The next emperor, Kao-tsung (650–683), if not himself a Christian, nevertheless continued to favour the new faith.   Then followed a period when Buddhism came into official favour, but a little later there was again an emperor favourable to the Christians, Yuentsung (713–755).   The then reigning emperor, at the time of the erection of the stone, Tih-tsung (780–783), is also described as friendly toward Christianity.

The stone was erected in 781, 'in the days of the Catholicus Hanan Ishua.'   It is interesting to note that Hananyeshu II died in 779; but this discrepancy in date is neither serious nor surprising.   Many of these dates are difficult to fix with any exactitude; and even if both dates are correct, it is not improbable that news of the death of Hananyeshu and the accession of Timothy I had not yet reached Sianfu.   News travelled slowly, and we know that some of the outlying Nestorian metropolitans and bishops only communicated with the patriarch at intervals of four or even six years.   The inscription ends with a list of the names and descriptions of 128 persons, most of whom are priests.   Among the more notable are Adam, Lingpao, Hsingtung, Sabranishu, and Jazedbouzid.   The descriptions are not easy to interpret, but Adam was apparently the metropolitan.   Some of the names are in Chinese characters and of Chinese form, while others are in Syriac character and form.   It may be that this implies that the Christian priesthood in China included both native and Persian elements; but it is probable that at least the metropolitans were almost always sent from Persia.

In addition to this historical matter the stone bears a eulogy and general description of the Christian faith. A few of the more interesting statements may be quoted: 'Behold the unchangeably true and invisible, who existed through all eternity without origin.' 'This is our eternal true Lord God, threefold and mysterious in substance.' 'The illustrious and honourable Messiah, veiling His true dignity, appeared in the world as a man.' 'A virgin gave birth to the Holy One in Syria.' The stone mentions the bright star that announced Christ's birth, and says Persians visited Him. It refers to a New Testament of twenty-seven[1] books, and to the sacrament of baptism. We gather from it that Christian priests turn to the east in praying, pray for both living and dead, shave their crowns, but wear beards.

References contemporaneous with this stone are few, but are not incompatible with it. Thus the Patriarch Salibazacha (714–726) ordained a metropolitan for China, presumably one of Alopen's successors; and the Patriarch Timothy I refers to the death of a metropolitan of China in 790. There are also references in a few Chinese documents[2] which bear out the story told on the stone. Thus a decree dating from 745 runs: 'It is long since the religion of the Scriptures of Persia spread through the Middle Kingdom. When they first built monasteries we gave them in consequence of their supposed origin the name of Persian. In order

[1] But the Syriac New Testament canon consisted of twenty-two books (see p. 188). This is an interesting discrepancy, and must be taken into account when considering the authenticity of the stone.
[2] Details are given by Robinson, *History of Christian Missions*, pp. 167–169.

that men may know their real origin, the monasteries
of Persia at the capitals are to be changed to monasteries
of Syria. Let those also in all the prefectures and
districts observe this.'

During the seventh and eighth centuries the official
Chinese attitude seems to have been one of benevolent
toleration. But in the ninth century the great spread
of monasticism began to be regarded as undesirable,
and steps were taken to curtail it. Thus in the time
of the Emperor Wu-tsung (840–846) a decree was
issued in the year 845 containing this order: 'As to
the monks and nuns who come under the head of
aliens, making known the religions of other countries,
we decree that over 3,000 Syrians and Muhufu [Mus-
lims] return to lay life and cease to confound our
native customs.' Wu-tsung was equally opposed to
Buddhism, and made 265,000 Buddhist monks and
nuns return to lay life. It was decreed that in the two
capitals only two monasteries were to be left in each
main street, with a limit of thirty monks to each house,
and in the provinces no monastery was to exceed
twenty inmates. The number of houses and inmates
permitted after restriction suggests that Wu-tsung may
have had good reason for desiring to check the monastic
tendency. Valuable within limits, an undue number
of religious houses may become an incumbrance to a
community instead of a help.

After the time of Wu-tsung, Christianity in China
seems to have steadily declined. Abul Faraj,[1] writing

[1] This Abul Faraj died in 1043, and was a Nestorian scribe. He is
not to be confused with Abul Faraj the Jacobite maphrian (1226–1286),
who is usually referred to as Barhebræus.

in 987, says that a Christian who had travelled extensively in China told him that there was not a Christian left in the whole country, and that the old church buildings were in ruins. Others also speak of ruined monasteries. Though Abul Faraj's Christian informant may not have discovered any Christians, there were probably still some there, for we have a reference to a Syrian monastery at Sianfu in 1076 and one at Chengtu at about the same time. Nevertheless, we may safely assume that during the tenth and eleventh centuries Chinese Christianity was at a very low ebb. It never became quite extinguished, however, and although there are no records to give us details, there must have been a revival during the twelfth and thirteenth centuries, as is evidenced by what Marco Polo and others found when they visited China in the second half of the thirteenth century (see p. 167).

This chapter may well conclude with a map showing the distribution of Nestorian churches at the time of their greatest diffusion. The middle of the tenth century has been chosen because that was the time when the Nestorian Church reached its zenith in the Caliphate. In other regions the date might be different, and not always easy to state with any certainty. Perhaps for Arabia the fifth century, for India the ninth, for Turkestan the thirteenth, and for China the eighth. But the tenth century probably gives as high an average level as any, and it will be seen from the map on p. 136 that in that century the Nestorian Church stretched, even if tenuously, right across Asia;

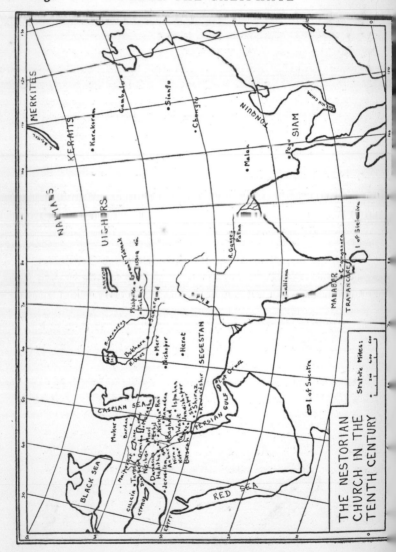

THE NESTORIAN
CHURCH IN THE
TENTH CENTURY

Statute Miles:

and Neale's assertion,[1] that 'it may be doubted whether Innocent III possessed more spiritual power than the Patriarch in the city of the Caliphs,' has some justification, if not in the number of communicants and degree of control, than at least in geographical extent.

PATRIARCHS OF SELEUCIA-CTESIPHON
650–1317

(This list is based on Kidd's interpretation[2] of Assemani. Wiltsch, also following Assemani, gives dates which are in most cases one or two years different from those of Kidd. The differences will usually only be noted if they exceed two years.)

Yeshuyab III, 650–660.[3]

Georgius I, 660–680.

John I, 680–682.

Hananyeshu I, 685–699.

VACANT, 700–714.[4]

Salibazacha, 714–728.

VACANT, 728–731.

Phetion, 731–741.[5]

Mar Aba II, 742–752.

Surinus, 754.

Jacob II, 754–773.

Hananyeshu II, 774–778.[6]

[1] *History of the Holy Eastern Church*, i. 143.

[2] *Churches of Eastern Christendom*, pp. 415–417.

[3] Wiltsch, *Geography and Statistics of the Church*, gives 655–664. For variants in the spelling of this and other names, see the supplemental index, pp. 223–227.

[4] The dates of the vacancies are given rather differently by Le Quien. See p. 107.

[5] Wiltsch gives 726–736.

[6] Fortescue, *Lesser Eastern Churches*, and Wiltsch give 774–779.

Timothy I, 778–820.[1]

Josue, 820–824.

Georgius II, 825–829.[2]

VACANT, 829–832.

Sabaryeshu II, 832–836.

Abraham II, 836–849.

VACANT, 849–852.

Theodosius, 852–858.[3]

Sergius, 860–872.

VACANT, 872–877.

Enos, 877–884.

John II, 884–892.

John III, 892–898.

John IV, 900–905.

Abraham III, 905–937.

Emmanuel, 938–960.

Israel, 962.

Ebedyeshu I, 963–986.

Mares, 987–1001.

John V, 1001–1011.[4]

John VI, 1013–1020.[5]

Yeshuyab IV, 1021–1025.

Elias I, 1028–1049.

John VII, 1050–1057.

Sabaryeshu III, 1063–1072.[6]

Ebedyeshu II, 1074–1090.

Machicha I, 1091–1108.

---

[1] Wiltsch gives 778–821, Fortescue and the *Encyclopædia Britannica* 779–823, and Browne, *Eclipse of Christianity in Asia*, 780–819.

[2] Wiltsch gives 825–832.

[3] Browne gives 852–868.

[4] Browne gives 1009 instead of 1011.

[5] Wiltsch gives 1012–1026, Browne gives 1012–1020.

[6] Fortescue gives 1057–1072, Browne gives 1061–1072.

Elias II, 1111–1132.

Barsuma, 1134–1136.

Ebedyeshu III, 1138–1147.

Yeshuyab V, 1148–1174. ——

Elias III, 1175–1189.[1]

Yaballaha II, 1190–1222.

Sabaryeshu IV, 1222–1225.

Sabaryeshu V, 1226–1257.

Machicha II, 1257–1265.

Denha I, 1265–1281.

Yaballaha III, 1281–1317.

THE PERFECT CALIPHS[2]

Abu Bakr, 632–634.

Umar I, 634–644.

Uthman, 644–656.

Ali, 656–661.

THE UMAYYAD CALIPHS OF DAMASCUS

Muawiyah I, 661–680.

Yazid I, 680–683.

Muawiyah II, 683–684.

Marwan I, 684–685.

Abdalmalik, 685–705.

Walid I, 705–715.

Sulayman, 715–717.

Umar II, 717–720.

Yazid II, 720–724.

Hisham, 724–743.

[1] Browne gives 1176–1190. Kidd has 'Elias IV,' which is surely an oversight or a misprint.

[2] The first three were formerly generally transliterated Abu Bekr, Omar, and Uthman.

Walid II, 743–744.
Yazid III, 744.
Ibrahim, 744.
Marwan II, 744–749.

THE ABBASID CALIPHS OF DAMASCUS

Abul-Abbas, 749–754.
Mansur, 754–775.
Mahdi, 775–785.
Hadi, 785–786.
Harun ar-Rashid, 786 809.
Amin, 809–813.
Mamun, 813–833.
Mutasim, 833–842.
Wathiq, 842–846.
Mutawakkil, 846–861.

After Mutawakkil the Abbasid Caliphs cease to be of much importance, and of the remaining twenty-seven only the dates of those mentioned in this work need be given:

Mutadid, 892–902.
Muktafi, 902–908.
Muqtadir, 908–932.
Qadir, 991–1031.
Mustasim, 1242–1258.

THE MONGOL GREAT KHANS

Jenghiz Khan, 1162–1227.
Ogdai, 1227–1241.
Kuyuk, 1241–1248.
Period of dispute, 1248–1251.
Mangu, 1251–1260.
Kublai Khan, 1260–1294.

Chapter VI

THE NESTORIAN CHURCH UNDER THE MONGOLS AND TIMUR

1258–1405

WHILE the Caliphate had been declining, a new power had been arising on its northern and eastern borders. The Mongols, first clearly emerging into history in the seventh century, had by the twelfth century become the greatest power in Asia. Under Jenghiz Khan (1162–1227) their sway extended from the Yellow River in China to the Dnieper, and during his time incursions south-eastward had already reached as far as Merv and Nishapur. The Caliphate, by now altogether lacking any effective cohesion or central authority, fell section by section under Mongol control, and the ancient Persian empire was thus becoming part of the Mongol empire, ruled from China by the Great Khans (Khakhans), the successors of Jenghiz Khan. The final subjugation was accomplished by Hulagu, brother of the Great Khan Mangu (1251–1260). Mangu, hearing that there were disorders in those parts of Persia which were already under the Mongols, sent Hulagu in 1251 to restore order; Hulagu did his work so thoroughly that by 1258 all Persia was

under his control. While Mangu lived, Hulagu was
content to act as governor of Persia, but when Mangu
died in 1260, Hulagu assumed the title ilkhan ('dependent khan'), and although owning a nominal
allegiance to the Great Khans in China, from that date
he was virtually independent ruler of Persia.

The effect of the Mongol conquest on the Christians
as such must be carefully distinguished from its effect
on them as inhabitants of conquered regions. The
Mongols were not hostile toward Christianity as a
religion until many years after the conquest of Persia
by Hulagu, but so ruthless were the Mongols in their
treatment of the regions which they overran that vast
numbers of Christians inevitably suffered in the
common fate. Few invading hordes can have inspired
such terror as did the Mongols. This was due to a
combination of astonishing mobility and relentless
ferocity. They were people of simple life, living in
tents and waggons, so that as communities they could
change their habitat much more readily than people
who had been accustomed to living in towns. Their
warriors were expert horsemen, and after an incursion
of mounted warriors it would not be long before a
whole community would follow on into the newly
opened territory.

It is little wonder that such methods inspired panic
among settled populations. The suddenness of their
attack is thus vividly pictured by Nau[1]: 'Clothed with
skins and riding the wind and tempest, they overturned

[1] Quoted by Stewart, *Nestorian Missionary Enterprise*, p. 257, from Nau,
L'expansion Nestorienne en Asie.

in the twinkling of an eye the strongest towns. They razed the walls and massacred their defenders. No sooner had news of their arrival been whispered abroad than without a moment's delay they seemed to spring up everywhere as if by magic. They covered the earth like the waters of a flood, and no one could resist them.' In many cases they reduced great cities to mere heaps of ruins, some of which never again recovered their former greatness. Indeed, some of the cities which they devastated virtually ceased to exist. Even allowing for exaggeration, accounts which have come down to us prove that a Mongol invasion was a disaster to be utterly dreaded.

Thus when Tule, youngest son of Jenghiz Khan, was sent to invade Khurasan, many formerly great cities were reduced to ruins. Merv, which he captured in 1221, was sacked and burned, and the number of slain has been estimated as between 700,000 and 1,300,000. From Merv he advanced to Nishapur, a great city of probably one and three-quarter million inhabitants. The Mongols spent fifteen days there, during which time the city was practically demolished, and all the inhabitants were slain – men, women and children – with the exception of 400 picked artisans, who were deported to Mongolia. The site of the city was afterwards sown with barley. Herat, at first spared because it opened its gates in immediate surrender, shortly afterwards shared a similar fate, because signs of insubordination were detected. For a whole week the Mongols slew and pillaged and burned, and 1,600,000 persons are said to have perished. Such accounts could be multiplied almost indefinitely,[1] and it is not to be wondered at that many Christian communities came to their end during the thirteenth century. When we find that the last mention of bishops or churches in certain places is dated in the first half of the thirteenth century, it may often be safely assumed that the church and the town perished together.

So far as Persia was concerned, the Mongol terror culminated in the sack of Baghdad by Hulagu in 1258. His procedure was true to the Mongol type. The Caliph Mustasim sued in vain for peace, finally coming in abject surrender to the camp of Hulagu. But it was all futile, for when Hulagu had made him deliver up all his treasure, he had him and his two sons slain. The city was then given up to plunder and pillage. Many notable buildings were destroyed, and the bulk of the population was massacred, Howorth estimating the dead as at least 800,000. In this case, however, the Christians received favour. They were all gathered together in one of the Baghdad churches, and Hulagu ordered that they should be spared. Incidentally, the fact that they were all able to take refuge in one church seems to show that their numbers at this time were sadly reduced, as the largest number we can imagine sheltering in this way could not exceed a few thousand.

This favour shown by Hulagu opened up a short period of Christian prosperity, and when Persia eventually became settled again under his rule, the Christians enjoyed a freedom that had never been

[1] For further examples of Mongol ferocity see Stewart, op. cit., pp. 256-270, Browne, *Literary History of Persia*, ii. 427-437, or Howorth, *History of the Mongols*, i. 78-101.

theirs before. Hulagu's tolerance seems to have been largely due to the fact that his wife, Dokuz Khatun, was a Christian. It is to be noted that although the formal religion of the earlier Mongol khans was Shamanism, a religion of primitive magic, Christian influences had been gradually affecting them for some centuries. This was partly due to the Nestorian missions which had already penetrated many parts of Turkestan, Mongolia and China (see pp. 127–135), and also to the fact that so many men of special knowledge were Christians. The Mongols were a people of little culture, so that Christian doctors, secretaries, and other officials were necessarily welcome among them. It is hardly to be doubted that by the time of the Great Khan Kuyuk there was quite a considerable Christian element among the Mongols, not only extraneous, but native. Although Jenghiz Khan and his son and successor, the Great Khan Ogdai (1227–1241), were certainly not themselves Christians, they seem to have been favourably disposed toward those who were, and full liberty of worship was allowed them. The next two Great Khans of importance,[1] Kuyuk (1241–1248) and Mangu (1251–1260), are, however, asserted to have been Christians themselves. Thus Barhebræus writes: '[Kuyuk] was a true Christian. His camp was full of bishops, priests and monks.' He employed Christians for the management of all affairs, and as doctors, and a Christian chapel stood before his tent. As to Mangu, Rashid describes him as

[1] There was an unsettled period between Kuyuk and Mangu, during which the successive Great Khans were Kaidu and Chapai.

'a follower and defender of the religion of Jesus.'
Assemani quotes Haithon to a similar effect. Hulagu,
therefore, even though not perhaps himself a Christian,
had come under a great deal of Christian influence in
addition to that of his wife. There is also reason to
believe that his mother, Sarkutti Bagi, was a Christian.
Other notable Mongol Christians whom we know by
name include Kaddak, Kuyuk's grand vizier, Bulgai,
Mangu's secretary, and Sigatsy, viceroy of Samarqand.

Thus it came about that when Hulagu had established himself in Persia, one of the first effects of the
new regime was a marked alteration in the status of
Christians. From being a subject melet they became
the most favoured religion, and it was the Muslims
who became subject to restriction. Hulagu gave a
palace of the former caliphs as a residence for the
Nestorian patriarch, and allowed a new church to be
built. Unfortunately, the Christians did not use their
newly won favour wisely. So long accustomed to
repression, when they became free they tended to treat
others as they themselves had been so often treated.
Thus Maqrizi, a Muslim historian, writes that the
Christians soon made others realize their new position:
'They produced a diploma of Hulagu guaranteeing
them express protection and the free exercise of their
religion. They drank wine freely in the month of
Ramadan, and spilt it in the open streets, on the clothes
of the Muslims, and the doors of the mosques. When
they traversed the streets bearing the cross they compelled the merchants to rise, and ill-treated those who
refused.' 'When the Muslims complained, they were

treated with indignity by the governor appointed by
Hulagu, and several of them were by his orders bastina-
doed.' Nor is the evidence only from the Muslim side.
The Armenian king Haithon, a Christian, says of
Dokuz Khatun, Hulagu's wife, that 'this devoted
Christian lady at once sought permission to destroy
the Saracens' [i.e. Muslims'] temples, and to prohibit
the performance of solemnities in the name of Muhammad, and caused the temples of the Saracens to be
utterly destroyed, and put the Saracens into such
slavery that they dared not show themselves any more.'
But Hulagu did not allow the Christians to have things
entirely their own way, and sometimes they suffered
for their excesses. Thus when the Christians of Takrit
plundered their Muslim neighbours, Hulagu ordered
all the Christians in Takrit to be slain, with the exception of the aged and the children, and their cathedral
to be handed over to the Muslims.

With one exception, Ahmad, the next five ilkhans
of Persia were all either Christians or favourably inclined towards Christianity. Thus Abagha (1265–
1280), Hulagu's successor, ordered that all clerks in
government offices should be either Christians or Jews,
but not Muslims. After Abagha came the short reign
of Ahmad (1280–1284), who was originally a Christian
but had become a Muslim. Islam was still unpopular
among the Mongols, and it was largely because of his
faith that Ahmad was deposed, and another Christian
ilkhan, Arghun (1284–1291), took his place.

But now a change of attitude began to evidence
itself among the Mongols. Some had become

Christians, a few had become Muslims, but most of them
had remained heathen.   Apart from those who had
become real Christians, the Mongols appear to have
had a genuine regard for Christianity.   This was based
upon two considerations: first, a respect for Christianity
as the faith of men of learning on whom they had come
to rely for the administration of practical affairs; and
second, the idea that as they were pitting themselves,
at least in the south-west, against people whose faith
was Islam, it would seem logical to identify themselves
with a faith which those people opposed, namely
Christianity, rather than with the faith of their enemies.
Irrelevantly to our way of thinking, but logically to
theirs, their victories were ascribed to the weakness of
Islam as a faith, and, by implication, to the desirability
of Christianity.   It is therefore to be feared that a good
many of those Mongols who became Christians did so
because they thought Christianity was the faith which
led to victory and success.

Nor are they to be altogether condemned for holding
that view, because Christians appear to have themselves
encouraged the idea.   Thus in a letter which Pope
Alexander IV is supposed to have sent to Hulagu when
he heard that Hulagu was thinking of being baptized,
the Pope says: 'See how it would enlarge your power in
your contests with the Saracens if the Christian soldiery
were to assist you openly and strongly, as it could,
with the grace of God.   You would thus increase your
temporal power, and inevitably also secure eternal
glory.'   The Pope seems to have overlooked the fact
that if Hulagu had been baptized, it would almost

certainly have been done by the Nestorian patriarch, so that he would have become merely a heretic and schismatic when that rite had been performed. On the other hand, the Pope may have been hopeful of getting Hulagu to submit to the Roman rite, in which case it would have been a signal triumph for Roman Catholicism. At the same time, we have to remember that during the Middle Ages it seems to have been overlooked that the Nestorian churches of Asia were excommunicate, and we have the extraordinary circumstance of a Nestorian envoy receiving Holy Communion from the Pope himself.[1] That was about 1288, a matter of little over a quarter of a century after the Pope's letter to Hulagu.

As, therefore, the adherence of the Mongols to Christianity was based, at least to a great extent, upon its worldly efficacy, it is hardly surprising to find a change of attitude when their prosperity in warfare began to wane. Indeed, the change over of the Mongols from favour towards Christianity to fanatical Muhammadanism seems only accountable on the assumption that they became convinced that Christianity was not a religion ensuring worldly success, and that Islam was therefore preferable. Conviction of this kind grows cumulatively; and the first indication that Islam was not synonymous with inevitable defeat was received in 1260, when the Mamluk Sultan of Egypt completely defeated the Mongols at the battle of Ain Jalut, between Nablus and Baissan. One result of this defeat was a persecution of Christians in Damascus, where

[1] See p. 153.

the Muslims, regaining the upper hand after their recent subjugation by Hulagu, made the Christians suffer for the arrogance they had displayed when they thought their position of superiority permanently assured. There was a similar reaction in Mosul two years later (1262) when the Muslims temporarily drove the Mongols out of that city. Many Christians were slaughtered.

Another test case was the rebellion of the Tartar chief, Nayan, against the Great Khan Kublai (1260–1294). Kublai Khan did not profess Christianity, whereas Nayan did. Nayan's rebellion failed, and he himself was slain in battle. The average Mongol concluded that if Nayan, a baptized Christian, bearing on his banner the sign of the cross, was thus worsted, the Christian faith was not a faith for conquerors. Christian apologists were not slow to point out that it could not be expected that God would favour one who was rebelling against his overlord, and, according to Marco Polo, Kublai Khan himself endorsed that argument. But the average Mongol more probably agreed with those whom Marco Polo quotes as saying, 'See now what precious help this God's cross of yours hath rendered Nayan, who was a Christian and a worshipper thereof!' This tendency to judge by results was also shown by Kublai Khan himself. Marco Polo records Kublai's answer to the question as to why he did not become a Christian; the answer is a long one,[1] but its tone and outlook is revealed in the first few sentences: 'How would you have me to become a Christian? You

[1] Given in full in Yule, *Travels of Marco Polo*, i. 339.

see that the Christians of these parts are so ignorant that they achieve nothing, whilst you see the idolaters can do anything they please.'

Nevertheless, the influence of a capable patriarch was still considerable. The outstanding patriarch during this period was Yaballaha III. He belonged to the Nestorian mission in China, which was enjoying a brief period of renewed vitality after becoming almost extinguished in the eleventh century. Unfortunately, the renewal was of brief duration (see p. 167), but if men of the quality of Yaballaha laboured there at that time, the work was excellent while it endured. Yaballaha evidently intended to make a pilgrimage to the Holy Land, and passed through Baghdad on his way. The patriarch at that time, Denha I (1265–1281), was so impressed by Yaballaha that he dissuaded him from going to the Holy Land, and wished him to return to China as metropolitan of Cathay and Wang. Whether this was intended to be additional to the metropolitan of China whose seat we assume to have continued at Sianfu, or whether it was intended to assign a new area to Yaballaha for missionary expansion, or whether it was merely a titular honour, is impossible to decide; for almost immediately afterwards Denha died, and Yaballaha was appointed patriarch. He governed the Church very prudently during a most difficult period (1281–1317). It was a time of increasing difficulty and anxiety in Persia, and the churches in other parts of Asia were mostly moving steadily to their decline. None the less, Yaballaha did what he could, and for the most part was able to maintain good relations with the ilkhans, particularly with Arghun (1284–1291). It was during the reign of Arghun that one of the rare contacts between the Nestorian Church and Western Christendom was established. The circumstances are fully related by Chabot,[1] but at least a brief summary may be given.

The ilkhan Arghun thought it might be of advantage to establish contact with Christianity in the West, and decided to send an embassage. Consulting Yaballaha as to whom to send, Rabban Sauma was selected, who was a monk Yaballaha had brought with him from China. Rabban Sauma accordingly set out, going first to Constantinople and then on to Rome. The Pope Honorius IV had just died (1287), but Sauma was received by the cardinals. They discussed matters of faith with him, and learned that his church had been founded by 'Mar Thomas, Mar Addai, and Mar Maris.' He recited the Nestorian creed to them, which was substantially the Nicene Creed. But he told them that Christ had 'two natures, two hypostases, and one person,'[2] and also that the Holy Spirit proceeded from the Father only. When the cardinals would have taken up these theological questions, Sauma very diplomatically told them that he had not come to argue, but to venerate the Pope. Pending the election of a new Pope, he visited Paris and saw King Philip IV, and went to Gascony and met King Edward I of England. Edward told Sauma that he was intending to fit out another crusade. He did not do so, however.

[1] *Histoire de Mar Jab-Alaha, Patriarche, et de Raban Sauma*, p. 60.
[2] On this, see p. 54.

Sauma then returned to Rome, and found the new Pope, Nicholas IV (1288–1292). Sauma showed him great reverence and received Holy Communion from him on Palm Sunday, 1288. He was also given leave to celebrate his own liturgy. During all this neither Pope nor cardinals seem to have realized that Rabban Sauma was a heretic and a schismatic! As to Sauma, he regarded the Pope as 'Catholicus and Patriarch of the western peoples,' just as Yaballaha was Catholicus and Patriarch of the East. This, incidentally, has always been the Nestorian attitude. They regard Christendom as divided into patriarchates, of which their own is one, and they regard the Pope as simply one of the patriarchs, perhaps senior by right of holding the see of St. Peter at Rome, but not entitled to jurisdiction over the others.[1] Shortly afterwards Rabban Sauma returned to Baghdad, laden with gifts and some precious relics, to report to the ilkhan Arghun and to the Patriarch Yaballaha the wondrous story of his adventures among the Christians of the West.

Unfortunately, shortly after this an event occurred which still further weakened the Mongol belief in Christianity as a religion leading to worldly success: the Muslims captured Acre, the final stronghold of the Crusaders. That was in 1291, and ended the Crusades. Not unnaturally, the Mongols regarded it as a victory of Islam over Christianity, and from that time onwards the Mongols steadily tended away from Christianity and towards Islam. At the time of the fall of Acre the last Christian ilkhan of Persia, Gaikhatu (1291–1295),

[1] The present patriarch approves this statement.

had just begun his reign. By the time he died, popular feeling had decidedly gone over to Islam. There were two claimants to the throne: Baidu, a half-hearted Christian, and Ghazan, a professing Muslim. The struggle did not last long; the great majority of the people went over to the side of Ghazan, and Baidu was slain.

This was a triumph for Islam, and inevitably the Christians were again reduced to a position of inferiority and subjection. The genuine Christian stock was a very small one, as was made evident when Hulagu took Baghdad nearly forty years before. The bulk of the indigenous population was Muslim, and at heart had remained so. It was therefore to be expected that now their Mongol rulers had embraced their own faith the pent-up antipathy of forty years would find expression. It did so, and as much from popular pressure as from his own desire, Ghazan began a fierce persecution of all Christians within his domains. Nauraz, one of his generals, appears to have been an enthusiastic leader of this persecution, and many of the edicts were issued in his name. One reads thus: 'The churches shall be uprooted, and the altars overturned, and the celebrations of the Eucharist shall cease, and the hymns of praise, and the sounds of calls to prayer shall be abolished; and the heads of the Christians, and the heads of the congregations of the Jews, and the great men among them, shall be killed.' In many places these orders were literally carried out. In others greater clemency was shown, and in return for substantial bribes persons and churches were

spared. Thus the churches at Erbil, both Nestorian
and Jacobite, were destroyed, because neither the
metropolitan nor his people could find the money to
redeem them. But at Mosul a great effort was made,
and, by selling all the church plate and ornaments,
as well as by generous personal gifts, destruction was
bought off. The sum raised, according to Assemani,
was 15,000 denarii. The Patriarch Yaballaha suffered
great indignities, including torture and imprisonment,
only being released on payment of a ransom of 20,000
dinars.

Practical help then came from the Armenian king,
Haithon. His generous gifts helped to buy off the
church at Maragha from destruction, and he began to
intercede with Ghazan to stop persecuting the Christians. Strangely enough, Ghazan yielded to this
persuasion, and issued an edict countermanding the
repressive measures against Christians and ordering
restoration of all plunder. He also gave the patriarch
5,000 dinars, presumably by way of compensation,
and treated him well during the rest of his reign. This
took place in 1296, so that officially the persecution
lasted rather less than a year. Outside Baghdad,
however, little was done in the way of restoration, and
in outlying provinces sporadic persecution still went
on. This is not surprising, as the popular spite against
Christianity was in no way diminished, and men like
Nauraz were only too ready to exploit it. Nevertheless,
Yaballaha continued to enjoy Ghazan's favour, and
was able to build a magnificent new monastery at
Maragha.

The general trend, however, was toward decline, and many churches are not heard of again after the thirteenth century. Thus the following churches are last heard of at the dates added after each: Destesana, 1260; Haditha, 1265; Maalta and Nuhadra, 1280; Susa, Arzun, and the island of Socotra, 1282. This does not imply that these churches ceased to exist in the years named. In some cases the decline may have been gradual, until the unpopular Christian minority gave up the struggle, either becoming Muslims or giving up religious practice altogether; in other cases the church may have come to its end during a local or general persecution, such as that under Ghazan and Nauraz in 1295. But it is certain that the thirteenth century witnessed a continued decline of Christianity in Persia.

Ghazan was succeeded by Uljaitu (1304–1916), whose general attitude was similar to that of Ghazan. He himself was tolerant and remained on friendly terms with the Patriarch Yaballaha. But he was unable or unwilling to prevent Muslim antipathy to the Christians breaking out in various parts of his kingdom, and there were several persecutions during his reign. According to the *Book of the Histories of Johannes of Dzar*,[1] there was a general persecution of a severe nature in 1306. The description is framed in such extravagant terms that we can hardly accept it as reliable in detail, but a few sentences from it may be quoted: 'Kharbanda Khan [i.e. Uljaitu], autocrat of the nation of the Archers, a wicked man, who hated

[1] Quoted by Browne, *Eclipse of Christianity in Asia*, p. 169.

the Christians, led away by sorcerers and heretical sheiks, and inspired by the wicked counsels of their assistant, Satan, began the struggle against the invincible rock of Christ. A decree was published in all the universe, referring to the Christians under his dominion, that they should adopt the stupid religion of Muhammad, or that each person should pay a kharaj tax of eight dahecans, that they should be smitten in the face, their beards plucked out, and should have on their shoulders a black mark.' 'Meanwhile the Christians remained faithful. They paid the exactions, and bore the torments joyfully. Kharbanda Khan, seeing that these means were insufficient, ordered them all to be made eunuchs, and to be deprived of one eye, unless they became Muslims.'

There appears to have been local persecution in Georgia in 1307, and there was a very serious outbreak of Muslim mob violence against the Christians in Erbil in 1310. There does not seem to have been any official responsibility for what happened at Erbil, beyond the fact that Uljaitu did not trouble either to investigate the causes of complaint or to take steps to prevent disorder when it threatened. The result was a grave loss of Christian life in Erbil, and the Patriarch Yaballaha, who was there at the time, barely escaped with his life.

Uljaitu was succeeded by Abu Said (1316–1335), during whose reign a disintegration of the Persian Empire took place very similar to that which occurred under the later caliphs. Powerful viziers and generals gradually gained authority in various localities, so that, when Abu Said died, the empire was virtually split up into about five independent units. The details are unimportant[1] from the point of view of Nestorian history, as after the time of Uljaitu we have very little information about the fortunes of the Nestorians during the fourteenth century. We can legitimately conclude that in such unsettled times they continued to suffer in various localities at the hands of the Muslims, no longer restrained by laws against the molestation of Christians. Indeed, if there had been such laws, they would hardly have been likely to be enforced in such disordered times.

Browne contends[2] that the list of patriarchs itself witnesses that the period was one of unsettlement, as the patriarchate was not only admittedly unoccupied for nine years (1369-1378), but the average length of reign after the death of Yaballaha in 1317 until the end of the fifteenth century was over twenty years. This is an appreciably greater average than heretofore, and Browne takes it to indicate that there were a number of vacancies glossed over by assigning to some of the patriarchs periods longer than their actual reigns. This may be so. On the other hand, by the end of the fifteenth century the patriarchate had become hereditary. This had arisen gradually, the practice being to appoint a nephew of the previous patriarch, at first, probably, by prior right if suitable, and later as a matter of course. This would mean accession at an earlier age, and may explain the longer reigns.

[1] For a concise summary see *Encyclopædia Britannica* (11th edition), xxi. 227. It is not given in the 14th edition.
[2] Op. cit., p. 172.

There is further evidence of continued decline in the disappearance of churches. The churches at Tirhana, Jundishapur, Balada, Dasena, Karkha, and Achlat are not heard of after 1318, and we may conclude that they became extinct during the unsettled times through which Persia passed after the empire of the ilkhans began to disintegrate. The churches at Beth-Bagas (till 1360), and Gesluna are last heard of a little later, but they also disappeared during the same period.

When, therefore, Timur i Leng (Tamerlane) began the conquest of Persia about 1380, it is improbable that Nestorian churches were to be found in many centres. Indeed, we can only say with certainty that there were churches at Baghdad, Mosul, Erbil, Nisibis, Bakerda (Gezira), Taurisium (Tabriz), and Maragha. There may have been a few others, particularly in the regions just north of Mosul and Nisibis; perhaps we might safely add to this list Amadia, Ormia (Urmi), Mardis, Amida (Diarbekr), and Maiperkat. But a comparison of this meagre list with that on pp. 123–124 will at once show what a lamentable decline had taken place in the Persian Nestorian Church since the time of its greatest influence. This fact needs to be borne in mind, because it is sometimes said that it was Timur who destroyed Nestorian Christianity. It may well be that his devastating campaigns sealed its fate, but its life was at a very low ebb before he came on the scene, and it was already concentrating into that area which was to be its only habitation for the next five hundred years.

Timur i Leng (i.e. Timur the Lame) was a Turk of

the Berlas tribe, who began his reign at Samarqand in 1369. Almost at once he began a policy of expansion and conquest, and swept about Western Asia in much the same way that the Mongols had done a century or two earlier under Jenghiz Khan and his successors. Timur gradually reduced the minor dynasties which had divided Persia, and by 1380 had subjugated Khurasan, and by 1392 Mesopotamia and Armenia, having captured Baghdad and Diarbekr. By 1395 it may therefore be said that the former Persian Empire was entirely under his sway, though as was inevitable in such large scale conquests there were many minor revolts. As Timur was a Muslim, Christians in the conquered territories would expect even worse treatment than other inhabitants. But as with the Mongol expansion, the terrors of invasion were usually equal for all, and there are many cases where Timur wiped out whole cities in much the same way as the Mongols had done. Thus Ispahan was devastated, 70,000 heads being piled up in pyramids as a monument of Timur's vengeance; Baghdad was treated in a similar manner, a pyramid of 90,000 heads being erected on its ruins. In these wholesale massacres it is little wonder that many of the feebler Christian churches which may still have been existing came to their end; and of those Christians who did survive, demoralized and unnerved by the terrors through which they had passed, the majority yielded to the forcible acceptance of Islam which was imposed on the wretched remnants.

The fortunes of those few who remained true to their faith are not easy to trace, but eventually the greater

number of them settled among those who were already
in Kurdistan. Their subsequent history will be de
scribed in the next chapter, but after Timur's devastation of Persia and the adjoining countries at the end
of the fourteenth century, Nestorian Christianity as
a force of any consequence ceased to exist.

Timur died at Otrar in 1405, on an expedition the
objective of which was the subjugation of China.

NESTORIAN CHURCHES OUTSIDE PERSIA

(i) *India.*

Though having little recorded history, the Indian
churches continued to maintain their work, for Marco
Polo, who travelled in the East from 1270 to 1295, says
that he found Christians and Jews in the kingdom of
Quilon (Travancore), and that there were six great
kingdoms in central India, three of which were Christian and three Saracen (Muslim). The tradition that
St. Thomas had been to India was well established by
the time of Marco Polo's visit, as he tells that many
pilgrims visited his tomb at Milapur. John of Monte
Corvino, who was sent by Pope Nicholas IV as special
missionary to China (see p. 167), on his way stayed for
some months in India, and says that he baptized several
hundred people in South India, and that the Church
of the Apostle St. Thomas was there. This would have
been about the year 1292.

Two other references from about the same period
are not, however, quite so optimistic. Menentillus, a
friar who visited India in 1310, says that he found

Lc

Christians and Jews in India, but that they were few in numbers, of little account, and subject to oppression; and Sir John Mandeville, who was in India perhaps a little later than Menentillus, says that he found a little Christian community of fifteen houses round the tomb of St. Thomas, consisting of Nestorian monks, whom he describes as 'recreant Christians and schismatics.' He also says that the body of St. Thomas had been taken to Edessa, but had been brought back to India again. (This view is still held at Milapur (Mylapore), and the tomb is shown in the nave of the Roman Catholic cathedral there. The more generally accepted tradition, however, is that his remains were never returned to Milapur from Edessa, but were taken from Edessa to the island of Chios in the Ægean Sea, and subsequently to Ortone in Italy, where they now repose.)

Reduced though it probably was, the Christian community in India lived on, and when Vasco da Gama visited the Malabar coast in 1498 he found 'Christians of St. Thomas' there, ruled by a metropolitan at Angamale. They still had some kind of touch with the Nestorian Church, for so late as 1503 the Patriarch Elias V sent three bishops, who reported that they found 30,000 Christians living mainly in two districts of South-West India. But distance and their pride in St. Thomas had already made these Indian Christians virtually a separate community, and after the sixteenth century we may reckon that they are no longer part of the Nestorian Church.

Their subsequent history merges into that of modern

Christian missions, the earliest of which were the six-
teenth-century missions of the Roman Catholics, most
notably under Francis Xavier, who went there in 1541.
Indeed, for a period after 1599 the Indian Church became Roman Catholic, but it broke away again later, and
since the end of the seventeenth century has no longer
been a unity. It has been divided between Jacobites
and Uniates, with two further subdivisions dating from
the latter part of the nineteenth century, when the
Thomas Christians broke off from the Jacobites (who
themselves again broke into two sections in 1909), and
the Syro-Chaldæans from the Uniates. The Syro-
Chaldæans represent a return to the Nestorian Church,
with which they maintain a nominal connexion. Their
metropolitan, Mar Timotheus, was consecrated by the
Nestorian patriarch in 1907. But the connexion is a
slender one, and the Nestorian patriarch's jurisdiction
over them is purely titular. These various sections of
the old Indian Church are often called 'Syrian,' as
indicative of their origin. Thus the Uniates are called
Romo-Syrians, the Jacobites Orthodox Syrians, the
Thomas Christians Reformed Syrians, and the Nestorians Syro-Chaldæans. Of these the Romo-Syrians
are the most numerous, numbering perhaps nearly
half a million, while the other three total about half a
million altogether. By far the smallest section is the
Syro-Chaldæan, who number about 8,000.

In so far as the term is in any way justifiable, these
South-West Indian Syro-Chaldæans are the one remaining missionary branch of the Nestorian Church.

(ii) *Turkestan.*

As was seen in the last chapter, there was in the twelfth century a considerable Christian element among the Tartar and Mongol tribes. Little more than the bare fact can be stated with any degree of certainty, but an interesting confirmation of the widespread distribution of Nestorian Christianity in central Asia is provided by the Christian graves which have been found in the province of Semiryechensk in Southern Siberia, which now forms part of the Union of Soviet Socialist Republics, but comes well within the area we have been denoting by the term Turkestan. These graves were discovered near the villages of Great Tokmak and Pishpek, both of which are at no great distance from Lake Issiq Köl.

They were discovered toward the end of the last century, and the inscriptions range from the years 1249 to 1345. The language used is in most cases Syriac, though some of the names are in a Turkish dialect. Full particulars of these stones and their decipherment are given by Chwolson[1] and Mingana.[2] There are several hundred of them, but it will be sufficient to give a few of the more interesting ones. The dates are those on the stones themselves, but reduced to years Anno Domini.

Dated 1255: 'This is the grave of the chorepiscopus Ama. He departed from this world in the month of

---

[1] *Mémoires de l'Académie Impériale de Sciences de St. Pétersbourg,* xxxiv. 4 and xxxvii. 8.

[2] *Bulletin of the John Rylands Library,* ix. 334–335.

July, on the Sabbath. May our Lord unite his spirit with those of the pious and upright.' A chorepiscopus was the bishop of a small town or village whose status was reckoned inferior to that of the bishops of larger towns and cities. Their powers were progressively restricted.

Dated 1272: 'This is the grave of the priest and general Zuma, a blessed old man, a famous Emir, the son of general Giwardis. May our Lord unite his spirit with the spirits of the fathers and saints in eternity.' This shows that, as was often the case in early times, the taking of Holy Orders did not preclude engagement in some other occupation, even soldiery, and that many of these Turkish Christians were men of position.

Dated 1307: 'This is the grave of the charming maiden Julia, the betrothed of the chorepiscopus Johanan.' A pathetic proof that there was no clerical celibacy, at least for orders up to chorepiscopus.

Dated 1315: 'This is the grave of Sabrisho, the archdeacon, the blessed old man and the perfect priest. He worked much in the interests of the Church.'

Dated 1326: 'This is the grave of Shliha, the celebrated commentator and teacher, who illuminated all the monasteries with light. Son of Peter, the august commentator of wisdom, his voice rang as high as the sound of a trumpet. May our Lord mix his pure soul with the just men and the fathers. May he participate in all heavenly joys.'

Dated 1338: 'This is the grave of Pesoha, the renowned exegetist and preacher, who enlightened all

cloisters through the light. Extolled for wisdom, and
may our Lord unite his spirit with the saints.'

From these inscriptions it is not difficult to conjure
up a mental picture of these two little Christian communities in medieval Turkestan. It is hardly to be
doubted that there were many others very similar to
them, but of which no trace has remained.

Thus, at the time of Jenghiz Khan and his successors,
the Christian religion was not much more unfavourably placed than any other. We have seen, however,
that the official Mongol attitude underwent a change,
until by the end of the thirteenth century the ilkhans
had gone over to Islam. How this came about in
Persia has already been traced, and although comparable details are not available, we may conclude
that Christianity suffered a similar decline, to the
advantage of Islam, throughout Central Asia. This
is scarcely to be wondered at, for in addition to the
other reasons which have been adduced, it is probable
that Islam is a form of faith having a greater appeal
to people of the Mongol type than has Christianity, at
any rate during times of aggressive expansion.

But in any case, the Turkestan churches were unfortunately in the track of the terrible Timur i Leng, and
after his career of devastation, lasting from 1369 till
1405, hardly a Christian church survived in Central
Asia. The fate detailed as befalling Christian communities in the Persian empire was, in all probability,
shared by the Christians of Turkestan, and accounts
for the disappearance of the once flourishing churches.
As in Persia, most of those Christians who were not

killed in Timur's massacres either openly apostatized
to Islam, or ceased to make open profession of their
faith. Details of the terrible cruelty of Timur's campaigns, and of his special cruelty toward Christians,
may be found in Huc, *Christianity in China*, or Price,
History of Muhammadanism.

Apart from the remnants in Persia and South-West
India, Timur's death in 1405 practically synchronized
with the extinction of Nestorian Christianity in Asia.

(iii) *China*.

In spite of the low state to which the Church in
China was reduced in the tenth and eleventh centuries,
a recovery undoubtedly took place. In the thirteenth
century men like Yaballaha and Rabban Sauma were
labouring there (see pp. 151–153), and travellers speak
of a quite strong Christian community. Thus Marco
Polo testifies to many Christians being in China in
1271, and some details are given about them by John
of Monte Corvino, who in 1289 was appointed by
Pope Nicholas IV as special missionary to China.
(Had this interest in the Far East any connection with
Rabban Sauma's visit to this same Pope the previous
year? See pp. 152–153.) John eventually arrived in
China in 1294, and laboured for many years in Cambalu (Pekin). In 1305 he sent a letter[1] to the Pope,
giving many interesting particulars of his own work,
and also some remarks about the Nestorians. He says
that they opposed his work: 'The Nestorians, certain
folk who profess the name of Christians, but who

[1] *The East and the West*, April 1904.

deviate sadly from the Christian religion, have grown
so powerful in these parts that they will not allow a
Christian of another rite to have ever so small a chapel,
or to proclaim any but the Nestorian doctrine.' He
claims to have baptized about six thousand converts
between 1294 and 1305, and says that but for the
Nestorian opposition the number would have been
nearer thirty thousand. This information is supple-
mented by John of Cora, who served in Cambalu for
a time under John of Monte Corvino. He also tells[1]
of the Nestorian opposition to the Roman mission, and
adds that the Nestorians somewhat resembled the
Greek Orthodox. He says that they numbered more
than thirty thousand, and were a rich community,
possessing very handsome churches. (It is curious that
John of Monte Corvino and John of Cora both
use the number 'thirty thousand.' Did the latter
misunderstand a reference by the former?)

The Nestorians and the Roman Catholic missionaries continued their work in opposition to one another
for nearly a century, when Christians of both persua-
sions alike were almost completely eradicated by the
intolerant and persecuting Ming dynasty, which had
gained control of China by 1369. Unlike the Mongol
successors of Kublai Khan, who, differing thus from
the Mongols who had gone westward, had remained
complacent toward Christianity, the Ming emperors
disliked all things foreign. Christianity was included in
this dislike, and the Nestorian Church in China came
to its end before the close of the fourteenth century.

[1] Yule, *Cathay and the Way Thither*, i. 238.

Christianity was almost, if not entirely, absent from China from that time until the commencement of modern missions, which for China may be reckoned as beginning with the Jesuits, who began work there towards the end of the sixteenth century.

THE MONGOL GREAT KHANS

Jenghiz Khan, 1162–1227.
Ogdai, 1227–1241.
Kuyuk, 1241–1248.
(Period of dispute, 1248–1251.)
Mangu, 1251–1260.
Kublai Khan, 1260–1294.

THE MONGOL ILKHANS OF PERSIA

Hulagu, governor, 1258–1260.
Hulagu, ilkhan, 1260–1265.
Abagha, 1265–1280.
Ahmad, 1280–1284.
Arghun, 1284–1291.
Gaikatu, 1291–1295.
Ghazan, 1295–1304.
Uljaitu, 1304–1316.
Abu Said, 1316–1335.

Chapter VII

THE NESTORIAN CHURCH IN KURDISTAN

1405–1914

DURING the unsettled years when the dynasty of the ilkhans was breaking up, and the still more troublous times of Timur, the place of residence of the patriarch changed frequently. When possible it seems that Baghdad was preferred, but when Baghdad was unsafe for him, he would take up his abode elsewhere. Thus the Patriarch Denha I (1265–1281), becoming dangerously unpopular owing to his severe treatment of a Christian who had apostatized to Islam, had to leave Baghdad in 1271 and take up his residence at Ashnu (modern Ushnu) in Azerbaijan. His successor Yaballaha III was often at Baghdad, but seems to have spent much of his time at Maragha, east of Lake Urmi in Azerbaijan. Mosul and Urmi were also frequent places of residence, and we find Baghdad being more and more forsaken in favour of places in the Kurdistan area. There were, however, periods of residence in Baghdad as late as the fifteenth and sixteenth centuries. It was only soon after the beginning of the nineteenth century that the patriarch again adopted a permanent seat, the village of Qudshanis, near the Great Zab, in Turkish Kurdistan.

After the death of Timur, the modern States of Turkey and Persia gradually consolidated themselves, and Islam has remained the official religion of the authorities ever since. Nestorian churches lingered on for some time in a few of the towns of Mesopotamia, but the region of their real strength tended more and more to become restricted to the part of Kurdistan between the Tigris and Lakes Van and Urmi, partly in Turkey and partly in Persia. Here they remained for the next five hundred years. The other centres died out at dates which cannot be exactly fixed, but an idea may be gained from their last mentions: Taurisium (Tabriz), 1551; Baghdad, 1553; Nisibis, 1556; Erbil, sixteenth century; Bakerda (Gezira), seventeenth century.

But even in their Kurdistan retreat the Nestorians did not remain free from either external or internal trouble. There were persecutions from time to time, and there have been disputes as to the succession to the patriarchate, such disputes sometimes leading to schisms. It has already been mentioned that the patriarchate tended to become hereditary (p. 158). As the patriarch could not marry, the succession passed from uncle to nephew. In 1551 this hereditary succession was challenged, with the result that the Nestorian Church became divided. The Patriarch Simon Bar-Mama died in 1551, and in the ordinary way would have been succeeded by his nephew, Simon Denha. In fact, a company of bishops duly proceeded to elect him; but some other bishops, supported by the heads of some of the chief families, wished to elect a

person whom they considered more suitable, John
Sulaka, a monk of the Rabban Hurmizd monastery.
They actually did so, and thus there were two in-
dependently appointed patriarchs. Sulaka thought
to strengthen his position by gaining the support of the
Roman Catholics, whose Franciscan missionaries were
already at work among the Nestorians. They readily
befriended him, sent him to Jerusalem, and thence to
Rome. There Pope Julius III (1550–1555) accepted
a Catholic profession of faith from him, and then
ordained him patriarch. This was in 1553, and
Sulaka thus became a Uniate. He then returned to
Kurdistan, hoping to gain over all the Nestorians to
himself. Had he succeeded, the history of the Nestorian Church would have ended with its reabsorption
into Rome. Unfortunately for Sulaka, however, two
years after his return he was imprisoned by the Pasha
of Diarbekr, and while in prison was murdered,
supposedly by the machinations of his rival, the
Nestorian patriarch of the old line. But Sulaka's line
did not lapse, and the Nestorian Church thus became
divided into two sections. Those who had re-established communion with Rome are usually described
as Uniate Chaldees. There were thus two lines of
patriarchs in Kurdistan, the Nestorian patriarchs of
the original succession, and the successors of Sulaka,
the Uniate Chaldæan patriarchs. The history of these
two lines during the next three hundred years reveals
that they exchanged rôles in a manner which must be
almost unique in ecclesiastical history.

The Uniate line, starting with John Sulaka (1551–

1555), was at first punctilious in retaining its standing with Rome. Sulaka's successor, Ebedyeshu (1555–1567), received the pallium from Pope Pius IV, and the next two, Aitallaha and Denha Shimun, seem also to have been truly Uniate. But subsequently touch with Rome became somewhat fitful. The people themselves were not in favour of any kind of control from Rome, and probably felt that it made little difference whether their patriarch was recognized by the Pope or not. Some of their patriarchs, therefore, sent a Catholic profession of faith to Rome, and a promise of obedience to the see of St. Peter; in return they received the pallium. Others did not trouble to do so. This irregular mode of procedure continued until 1670, when Mar Shimun XII sent the last such profession. (After the first few, all patriarchs of this line have adopted the name Mar Shimun.) After Mar Shimun XII, all relationship with Rome ceased, except that in 1770 the then patriarch wrote to Pope Clement XIV expressing a desire to restore the union. But nothing was done, and as the great majority of the ordinary clergy and laity had never appreciated the difference communion with Rome made, the Uniate Chaldees drifted back into schism. As theologically they had never really changed, except in the matter of the patriarchs' professions, after Mar Shimun XII the patriarchs of the Sulaka line are again Nestorian. Indeed, the succession of Nestorian patriarchs from Mar Shimun XIII onwards must be reckoned through the Sulaka line, as the old line became Uniate.

This came about during the end of the sixteenth

and beginning of the seventeenth centuries. The
patriarchs of the old line had also adopted a uniform
name. This was done soon after the dispute between
Simon Denha and John Sulaka, the name chosen
being Elias. This line began negotiations with Rome
during the time of Pope Sixtus V (1585–1590), the
Patriarch Elias V sending him a profession of faith.
This, however, was rejected on the grounds that it was
tainted with Nestorianism. But in 1607 Elias VI sent
a profession which was acceptable, and was received
into union; so also was his successor Elias VII in 1657.
It thus came about that both lines were Uniate during
the middle of the seventeenth century, there being a
Uniate Chaldæan patriarch of Sulaka's line at Urmi,
a Mar Shimun, and a Uniate Chaldæan patriarch of
the old line at Mosul, an Elias. But after Elias VII the
old line gradually ceased to keep its union with Rome,
and fell back into schism and Nestorianism, just as
Sulaka's line had done. In the eighteenth century
there were, therefore, two rival Nestorian patriarchs,
one at Urmi and one at Mosul. Yet there was still
evidently a section which regarded union with Rome
as desirable, and now that both lines were again in
schism, Joseph, metropolitan of Diarbekr, felt justified
in renouncing his allegiance to Elias VIII and applied
to the Pope for recognition. The Pope received him
at Rome and appointed him Uniate patriarch of the
Chaldees. At the latter part of the eighteenth century
there were thus three Chaldæan patriarchs: two Nestorians, at Urmi and Mosul respectively, and a Uniate
at Diarbekr. This state of affairs did not last long,

because in 1826 the old line at Mosul again became
Uniate, so that there was no longer any need to
continue the Uniate patriarchate of the Joseph succession. From that date, therefore, the old line has to
be called Uniate Chaldæan, the patriarchs of the Elias
succession being in communion with Rome; whereas
the newer line, the Mar Shimuns of Urmi, originally
Uniate, thenceforward must be taken to represent the
Nestorian patriarchate.

Fortescue[1] is therefore quite justified in pointing
out that the present names are not altogether historically justifiable: 'Mar Shimun, then, claims to represent
the old line of the Persian Katholikoi of Seleucia-
Ctesiphon from Mari and Papa Bar Aggai. His claim
is not true. Really he represents the line of patriarchs
founded by Sulaka, originally Uniate. The old line is
that of the present Uniate patriarch. Logically, then,
it should be said that the old Nestorian Persian Church
(represented by her hierarchy) is now Uniate, that
Mar Shimun is head of a schism from that Church
which has gone back to Nestorianism. That is
what anyone would admit, were no controversial
issue at stake. But since the rôles of the lines of
Sulaka and of Bar-Mama have now become so
curiously reversed, non-Catholics ignore their origin,
treat Mar Shimun as head of the old Persian (or
"Assyrian") Church, and the real old Church as
schismatic, because it is not in communion with
him.'

The facts are certainly as Fortescue says, though no

[1] *Lesser Eastern Churches*, p. 129.

particular 'controversial issue' seems to be 'at stake'; for it has to be remembered that Sulaka was ordained and appointed by Nestorian bishops before he received any Papal authority. The succession has, therefore, been in an unbroken line; and in any case it is obviously desirable to call the present successors of Elias Uniate Chaldees and the Mar Shimuns Nestorians, so that their present allegiances and positions may be made clear. Soon after 1826 the Nestorian patriarch moved from Urmi to Qudshanis, where his seat remained until the Great War (1914–1918).

Apart from this matter of the rival patriarchs, there is little to record in the history of the Nestorian Church between the end of the fifteenth and the beginning of the nineteenth centuries. They simply continued to exist, their sphere of influence reduced to a triangle whose corners were Lake Van, Lake Urmi, and Mosul, with a few scattered churches elsewhere in Kurdistan and Mesopotamia. As with all melets under Muslim rule, they suffered occasional persecution, their principal oppressors being the savage Kurds of Eastern Asia Minor. So far as the official Turkish attitude was concerned, such persecutions were not countenanced; but unfortunately the Sublime Porte had little control over the fierce tribes of its remoter districts, and Kurdish incursions were all too frequent, no doubt reducing the Nestorian remnant still further.

But at the beginning of the nineteenth century practical interest in the Nestorian Church was revived by the 'rediscovery' of this little Christian community by Claud James Rich in 1820. Mr. Rich was an

official of the East India Company, stationed at
Baghdad. He was also a keen archaeologist, and it was
his explorations around Nineveh that brought him into
touch with the Nestorians. Although the Roman
Catholics had been at work among them to a greater
or less extent for centuries, it was only after Mr. Rich's
contact with them that English and American Protestant missionary societies took any interest in them.
They then began to do so with great zeal, partly, no
doubt, owing to the fascinating nature of the problem.
Here were Christians speaking Syriac, a language
closely akin to that spoken by our Lord Himself;
Christians who had maintained their faith for over a
thousand years as an island community in a sea of
Islam; a Christian Church whose history went back
far before the Reformation, which yet owned no
allegiance to the Pope; a Christian Church which in
some superficial ways might even be called an Eastern
Protestantism.

Mission work thereupon began. The honour of
being the first worker should perhaps be conceded to
the Rev. Joseph Wolff, who went out from England
and obtained a copy of the Syriac New Testament.
He brought it back to England, where a printed edition
of it was prepared by the British and Foreign Bible
Society. When this was ready, in 1827, it was distri-
buted in great numbers round Urmi. Another immediate advantage of this increased interest in the
Nestorians was that when another Kurdish attack was
made upon them in 1830 protests were made to Turkey
by some of the European governments. The Turks

Mc

sent Rashid Pasha to set things in order, and by 1834 he had restored some degree of tranquillity. But it was unfortunately by no means permanent, as when the Turkish troops were withdrawn the hill tribes soon tended to revert to their old ways, and there was another massacre in 1842.

Meanwhile the American Presbyterians had entered the field, sending two missionaries, Messrs. Smith and Davies. They sent Dr. Julius Davies to help them in 1834, and Dr. Asahel Grant in the following year. This American Presbyterian Mission continued without interruption until the war, having its headquarters at Urmi.

The Church of England next took action through the Society for Promoting Christian Knowledge. They sent Mr. Ainsworth in 1842 to make inquiries, and he was shortly followed by the Rev. George Percy Badger, who was sent out under the auspices of the Archbishop of Canterbury (Dr. Howley) and the Bishop of London (Dr. Bloomfield). Mr. Badger only stayed a year, but during that time he created a good impression upon the Nestorians. He made it clear to them that the wish of the Church of England was simply to help them in all possible ways, but not to make them give up their old faith or order. For this reason the Nestorians have ever since been specially favourable towards the Anglicans. While Mr. Badger was among them there was another terrible Kurdish incursion, the massacre of 1842 referred to above. Sweeping down on the Nestorian villages, the Kurds carried off many women and children as captives, and over ten thousand persons were estimated to have been killed. Mr. Badger was able to shelter the patriarch, thus probably saving his life.

The work of Mr. Badger was not followed up for some years, until in 1868 the Nestorians sent a request to the Archbishop of Canterbury (Dr. Tait) for more help. In response to this appeal the Rev. E. L. Cutts was sent out to investigate, but not until 1876. The result of Mr. Cutts's inquiry was the establishment of the Archbishop of Canterbury's Mission to Assyrian Christians, which began in 1881 with the despatch of the Rev. Rudolph Wahl. He served till 1885, but does not seem to have been quite suited to the work. In 1886 three more missionaries were sent, Canon Maclean, Mr. Athelstan Riley, and the Rev. W. H. Browne. The mission continued from that time without interruption until the Great War. Its head-quarters were at first at Urmi, but in 1903 they were moved to Van, on the Turkish side of the frontier. Among their more recent workers one of the best known is Canon W. A. Wigram, D.D.,[1] who laboured there from 1902 till 1912. It may be remarked that the name chosen by the Church of England for its mission has tended to come into general use, and the Nestorian Christians are usually now referred to as Assyrians. No doubt the Anglican intention was to emphasize the ancient lineage of this Eastern Church, and perhaps to minimize any suggestion of heresy that the word Nestorian might involve. As their object was to

[1] To whom I am personally indebted for some of the facts in this chapter and the next.

'reform the Church from within,' there is much to be said for that point of view.

Among other missionary societies which also entered the field, mention must be made of the Danish Lutherans, the Norwegian Lutherans, the Baptists, and the Russian Orthodox. The success of the Russians was very fitful. So far back as 1827 quite a number of Nestorians fled from Kurdistan to Erivan in Russia, and became Orthodox. The Nestorians also sought Russian help in 1898, when a Nestorian bishop and four other clerics went to St. Petersburg (Leningrad) and declared that their Church would become Orthodox in return for Russian help and support. Russia accepted the challenge, and by 1900 they had built an Orthodox church at Urmi and set up a system of parishes and schools. For a little while it seemed as though the Nestorian Church was to be absorbed into the Russian Orthodox; but either the Nestorians did not receive all the advantages they had hoped for, or Russian zeal flagged. In any case, the Russian ascendancy was shortlived, in a very few years things were back where they had been, and Russian influence never counted for much again.

Details of the work of these various missions may be found in the publications of the societies concerned. But something must be said concerning the nature of their common problem: how should one deal with an ancient Church whose general condition, administrative, cultural, and doctrinal, was so unsatisfactory? The Roman solution is to make the Church Uniate, permitting it to keep its own rites and ceremonies in so

far as they are doctrinally unexceptionable, but otherwise making them conform to Roman canon law. The
Russian Orthodox solution would have been simply
to add the Nestorian Christians to their own communion, so that the Church as a separate entity would
have ceased to exist. But the attitude of the Anglicans
and of the other Protestant missionary societies did not
lead to such a simple solution. Their desire was to
preserve this ancient Church as an entity, so that it
might still reckon itself as the continuation of the
Church of the Persian Empire, and yet to free it from
ignorance, from erroneous doctrine, from maladminis-
tration, and from those other defects, major and minor,
which were the legacy of its stormy history. If the
Nestorian Church could have been reconstituted on a
sound basis, with regard to doctrine, administration,
and general efficiency, no doubt Protestant opinion
would have been satisfied. But until that could be
accomplished, it was imperative that they should
maintain their own organizations. This sometimes
resulted in a confused allegiance. Should a Nestorian
who admitted he owed much to, say, Norwegian
Lutheranism, forsake his historic Church to join the
Lutherans? On the other hand, he could not fail to
recognize that Lutheranism had much to offer him
which Nestorianism could not. Cases therefore sometimes arose like that of Nestorius George Malech, which
Fortescue quotes with obvious delight.[1] Malech was
an archdeacon of the Nestorian Church, and also the
authorized Norwegian missionary at Urmi, pledged to

[1] Op. cit., p. 121.

'remain true to the evangelical Lutheran confession.'
Naturally, granting its premises, the inexorable logic
of Roman Catholicism could never countenance such a
quandary; but Protestants will appreciate how difficult,
with rather different views of the Church, the position
was bound to be.

None the less, in spite of the delicacy of some of the
problems involved, it must be emphasized that all these
missions, Catholic, Orthodox, Anglican, and Protestant
alike, wrought great benefit to the Nestorians, both by
encouraging general education, distributing Bibles and
other religious books, establishing schools and hospitals,
and by improving the attitude of the Turkish and
Persian authorities toward a formerly little considered
melet; and it is probable that the Nestorian Church
grew both in numbers and in spiritual strength during
the latter part of the nineteenth century and the earlier
years of the twentieth.

Once more, however, the Nestorian Church was to
suffer the calamity of ruthless warfare. Just as the wars
between the Persians and the Arabs, between the
Caliphate and the Mongols, and between the Mongols
and the Turks had involved the Nestorian Christians
in suffering and slaughter, so also did the Great War of
1914–1918. Again they became victims of circumstances which were completely beyond their control.
A summary of their fortunes since 1914 will be given
in the concluding chapter, but it will perhaps be best
to describe their hierarchy, faith, and practice as they
existed in Kurdistan just before the war, rather than to
attempt to describe their present condition in those

respects.   Evidently we cannot describe the settled
institutions of a people who are not yet certain where
their future home is to be, nor can we expect a clearly
defined theology from a people whose primary concern
is their very existence.   If they become safely established in Iraq, or if some other more suitable habitat is
found for them, in ten years' time it may be possible
to give an accurate account of their hierarchy, their
theology, and their general practice.   In their present
unsettled state that is not possible, so it will be best to
set out what was the state of affairs in the years just
prior to the Great War.   This can most conveniently
be done under three main headings:

(1) *Extent and administration.*

The ecclesiastical centre of the Nestorian Church in
Kurdistan in the years immediately preceding the war
was the little village of Qudshanis, the residence of the
patriarch.   The village is near the Great Zab, just
inside the Turkish boundary.   The only towns of any
importance where Nestorians were to be found were
Urmi, Van, and Amadia, but they also inhabited many
villages in the plain round Lake Urmi, and in the
mountainous country, the Hakkiari, between Lakes
Urmi and Van.   Some were to be found in Mosul,
Diarbekr, and even in Urfa (Edessa), but these were
really out of the real Nestorian area, being districts
where Christianity was more represented by Jacobites
and Uniates.   As to numbers, an estimate is difficult,
various investigators giving very different totals.

Perhaps 100,000 may be somewhere near the truth.[1]

The hierarchy consisted of the patriarch, one metropolitan, and ten bishops. An episcopal diocese in the neighbourhood of Qudshanis was under the direct supervision of the patriarch. The metropolitan, now called the matran, controlled a diocese partly in Turkey and partly in Persia, and had his seat at Neri. Of the ten bishops, seven had dioceses on the Turkish and three on the Persian side of the frontier. These dioceses were ill defined, and not delimited with any precision. Under each bishop were several chorepiscopi (cf. p. 165). Each of these was responsible for a group of villages, the priests from which he assembled twice a year for direction and instruction. The chief chorepiscopus of the diocese was called the archpriest, and sometimes deputized for the bishop. In the village church the priest might be assisted by deacons, subdeacons, and readers. There were thus nine orders: patriarch, matran, archpriest, chorepiscopus, priest, deacon, sub-deacon, reader. There was an ordination ceremony for transition from each of these orders to the next. In addition to these nine orders there was for each bishop an archdeacon, whose duties were mostly secretarial and financial.

The priests were chosen by the community, subject to approval and ordination by the bishop. Normally a priest could not rise above the rank of archpriest, as the hereditary principal (uncle to nephew) had become customary, not only for the patriarch, but also for the

[1] So Fortescue, op. cit., p. 128, following Cuinet. Tozer gives 18,000, Petermann and Kessler 70,000, Silbernagl 150,000, and Yohanan 190,000.

matran and bishops. The only way in which a priest might become a bishop was when a bishop died leaving no relative eligible to succeed him. In that case a suitable priest would be chosen for the bishopric. Otherwise the episcopate remained in a closed group of families.

Since the early part of the seventeenth century the patriarch has always assumed the name Mar Shimun on accession, the personal name, when used, being inserted between Mar and Shimun. Thus the patriarch Mar (Reuben)[1] Shimun XVIII, who died in 1903, was succeeded by Mar (Benjamin)[2] Shimun XIX, who became patriarch at the age of seventeen. Mar Shimun XIX came to a tragic end in 1918, when he was murdered by a Turk named Ismail Agha Shekak, otherwise known as Simko. Hereditary names have also become customary for the matran and bishops. Thus the matran is always Mar Hananyeshu. Owing to the youth of Mar Shimun XIX, the matran, the venerable and experienced Mar (Isaac) Hananyeshu was conceded an almost equal respect and power. As to clerical celibacy, the patriarch, the matran and the bishops have to be celibates, but the other orders may marry. In the event of a wife's death, remarriage is permitted.

(2) *The Nestorian Faith.*

The Nestorian Christians call themselves simply Christians or Syrians, but if wishing to distinguish themselves from members of other Churches, they use the term Christians of the East. They do not like the

[1] Ruwil, Rubil.   [2] Benyamin.

term Chaldæan, using that for Uniates, but they do not
object to being called Nestorians. They hold that
they represent one of the five ancient patriarchates,
which they reckon as Rome, Alexandria, Constantinople, Antioch, and Seleucia-Ctesiphon (but cf. pp.
46–49). Their attitude toward the other ancient
Christian Churches is therefore independent but not
hostile. The Pope regards them as heretics and schismatics; but they regard him simply as the patriarch of
another section of the Church, entitled to rank with
their own patriarch, but to whom they are not willing
to concede either obedience or the headship of the
whole of Christendom.

Theologically, their ideas are vague. They recognize the first two Œcumenical Councils, Nicæa
(325) and Constantinople (381), and also certain
decisions of later Councils. In addition to this they
acknowledge the decisions of the Eastern Synods, the
various councils held under their own ancient Catholici
and Patriarchs. The generally recognized collection
of this body of canon law is that made by Ebedyeshu,
metropolitan of Nisibis (ob. 1318); but while probably
admitting its authority, it is doubtful whether there is
a modern Nestorian who has a real grasp of this body
of canon law and its implications. But they are clear
that they are committed to the teaching of Nestorius,
whatever that may have been, and that the Council
of Ephesus, Cyril of Alexandria, and the word Theotokos are three things utterly execrable. Thus on the
feast of the Greek Doctors (Diodorus, Theodore, and
Nestorius), which is on the fifth Friday after Epiphany,

they repeat these anathemas: 'Woe and woe again to all who say that God died, who say that Mary is the mother of God, who do not confess Christ in two natures, two persons, and one parsufa of filiation. Woe and woe again to the wicked Cyril and Severus.'[1] Apart from this formal and verbal adherence to Nestorius, which is probably more a loyalty to a person and a tradition than to an idea, their general belief is not greatly different from that of the rest of Christendom. With regard to this specific anathema, it is of interest to notice that Mar (Isaac) Hananyeshu expressed himself as willing to consider its suspension. That would have been a big advance.

For the rest, they believe in grace, free-will, and the value of good works. They pray for the dead, and honour relics and dust from the tombs of the saints; but they do not approve of sacred pictures or images, and make no use of crucifixes. They use crosses, however, respecting this symbol greatly. They consider that there are seven Sacraments, but it is not quite clear what they are. The Patriarch Timothy II (1318–1360) gave the following: (1) Holy Orders. (2) The Consecration of a church and altar. (3) Baptism and Holy Oil (Confirmation). (4) The Holy Sacrament of the Body and Blood. (5) The blessing of monks. (6) The Office for the dead. (7) Marriage. But he adds as a supplement, 'Indulgence, or penance and the forgiving of sins.' It seems that in addition to these they regard also as Sacraments: (1) The Oil

---

[1] Badger, *The Nestorians and their Rituals*, ii. 80. On the Christological terms, see p. 54 above.

of Unction (Extreme Unction). (2) The Holy Leaven.
(3) The Sign of the Cross. Although their liturgical
books contain a form for confession, it is hardly ever
used. It is said to have become obsolete because the
priests could not maintain sufficient secrecy. Their
creed is practically the Nicene Creed, of course without
the 'filioque' addition.

As to the Bible, under missionary influence they
were tending to accept and use the canon of Western
Christendom,[1] though the true Syriac canon is somewhat smaller. Ebedyeshu, metropolitan of Nisibis,
gives: the Four Gospels, Acts, the Epistle of James,
1 Peter, 1 John, fourteen Epistles of Paul (inclusive of
Hebrews). He also adds the Diatessaron of Tatian.[2]
The most significant omission is the Apocalypse.
Ebedyeshu's list, apart from his apparent re-
authorization of the Diatessaron, is the same as the
canon of the Syriac Peshitta, which dates from about
420.

(3) *Services, rites, and ceremonies.*

The Nestorian churches of Kurdistan were un-
interesting from the architectural standpoint, being
mostly small plain structures. Probably the best
building was that at Mosul. Many of them were,
however, of considerable antiquity, and thus attractive

[1] That is, for private reading and study. Lectionaries and liturgies
draw only from the Syriac canon.
[2] A composite gospel compiled from the canonical four, which was
prepared by Tatian, an Assyrian Christian, towards the end of the
second century. It remained in general use in Edessa and West Persia
till about the beginning of the fifth century, when it was superseded by
Syriac versions of the usual four.

archæologically. They were presumably intentionally plain in order to be inconspicuous, and so less likely to attract Muslim attention. The only indication of their nature was usually a plain cross above the door, which the worshippers kissed as they entered. The doors were generally very low, so, it was said, that all who entered should be obliged to bow in reverence. Fortescue suggests that a more probable reason was to prevent Kurds desecrating the churches by driving their cattle into them.[1]

The churches were more interesting inside than out. The nave was divided from the sanctuary by a wall, which had an arched opening in it about five feet wide. This opening could be closed, either by a curtain or, in some cases, by doors. The part of the nave in front of the sanctuary was separated off by a low wall broken in the middle, and was raised above the level of the rest of the nave, as was also the sanctuary itself. Against this dividing wall were placed tables for the service books, and on one of them stood a large cross. The ordinary services were conducted entirely in the nave, the choir standing just in front of the dividing wall. Inside the sanctuary was a raised platform under a canopy, and on this platform stood the altar, usually furnished with a plain cross, two candles, and the gospel book. As a link with very ancient history, it is of interest to remark that the sanctuary was called the Holy of Holies, in Syriac 'qdush qdushe,' which is not far from the original Hebrew 'qodesh haqqodoshim.' The baptistery was a separate room opening out of the nave, with

1 Op. cit., p. 145.

sometimes another door into the sanctuary. It was also used as a vestry, and often contained the oven for baking the bread to be used in the Eucharist. The churches usually bore the name of an apostle, saint, or martyr, and not infrequently of the Virgin Mary (*Mart Maryam*, 'Lady Mary').

The clergy did not wear distinctive dress, apart from a black turban, nor did they wear a tonsure. But they were always bearded; to be clean shaven was a sign of disgrace, sometimes inflicted by the bishop as a punishment on an erring priest. When officiating, however, vestments were used, similar in general to those of the Roman and Greek Churches, but simpler and less systematized. They included items corresponding to the alb, stole, cope, and amice. They had no chasuble, the cope serving the double purpose. Bishops carried a staff and a small cross.

As to services, every day there was morning and evening prayer, to which the worshippers were summoned by striking a kind of wooden gong with a hammer, though under missionary influence bells were increasingly coming into use. The worshippers removed their shoes on entering the church, but the turban or tarbush was only removed during the actual time of service. Their orders of service were not well defined, as quite a number of different service books were in use. It seemed to be left very largely to the priest's discretion. But in any case morning and evening prayer would include, not only psalms, collects, and responsive prayers, but also hymns and anthems. As with service books, they had quite a variety of hymn

and anthem books The services throughout were in
classical Syriac.

The Eucharist was not celebrated every Sunday, but
only on the chief feast days. Usually it took place in
the morning, but sometimes in the afternoon. Communicants should have fasted since midnight. Here
again there was no fixed order, as at least three rites
were in use. The most general was one which they
called the rite of the Apostles. Most liturgiologists
consider that this rite is a much modified form of the
Antiochene rite, passing into the Nestorian Church
via Edessa. Some, however, think it should be classed
by itself, considering that it contains too many other
elements to be reckoned in any real sense Antiochene.[1]

The rite began with the making of the bread, which
had to be mixed with Holy Leaven. This was supposed
to trace back to the Last Supper, and to have originally
been prepared from a loaf given by our Lord to St.
John, who mixed it with some blood from the Cross
and some water which had been saved from Christ's
baptism. This was then ground up, mixed with flour
and salt, and divided among the apostles. A little of it
was used with each baking of bread for the Eucharist,
and once a year, on Maundy Thursday, what was left
was renewed by the admixture of fresh flour, salt and
oil. The Nestorians believed that they alone had kept
up this continuity.[2] When all was ready the service
began. There was usually the Gloria in Excelsis, the

[1] So Baumstark, Renaudot, and Brightman.
[2] The Holy Leaven has not been lost despite the catastrophes of
recent years.

Lord's Prayer, some psalms, and an anthem. Then two lessons were read, one from the Old Testament and one from the Acts. After another psalm, a portion was read from the Apostle (i.e. from a Pauline epistle). Then there was another anthem, a reading from the Gospels followed by a short sermon or homily, another anthem, the Nicene Creed (without 'filioque'), and some responsive prayers. Then followed the act of communion. It was administered in both kinds, the priest giving the bread and a deacon the chalice. The service ended with the blessing.[1] The Eucharist was not reserved, and there was no provision for communion of the sick.

The baptismal service was a long one, and like the Eucharist was only conducted on feast days. Many children were therefore baptized at the same service, private baptism not being allowed. But as a mitigation of the often long period between birth and the next general baptism, soon after birth the child was washed in water that had been blessed by the priest. This ceremony was called 'signing,' and at it the child was given its name. At the actual baptism the child was anointed all over with olive oil, and was dipped three times in the font, being held so that it faced east. The priest said: '[Name] is baptized in the name of the Father, in the name of the Son, in the name of the Holy Ghost, for ever.' Confirmation followed at once, by the laying on of the right hand.

The marriage and burial services were also long, in

[1] For a more detailed description see Fortescue, op. cit., pp. 149–156, or Maclean and Browne, *The Catholicos of the East*, pp. 247–265.

some ways resembling the Greek Orthodox. In marriage the bride and bridegroom had threads of red, blue and white placed on their heads, corresponding to the Greek crowns. The burial service differed for clergy and laity, and special anthems were provided to cover all kinds of cases.

Their Church Calendar included many feasts and fasts. The most important feasts were Easter, Christmas, and Epiphany. They had a Great Fast corresponding to Lent, a fast before Christmas, one in honour of the Virgin Mary in August, and a three days' fast in the early spring to commemorate Jonah preaching to the Ninevites. There were numerous saints' days, with orders of service modified appropriately. Most saints' days fell on Fridays.

Chapter VIII

THE NESTORIAN CHURCH IN EXILE

1914–1936

Once again the Nestorians have been the victims of an international upheaval for which they were in no way responsible. In 1914 the outlook seemed encouraging. The various missionary societies, notably the Archbishop of Canterbury's Mission to Assyrian Christians, were doing valuable work, so that the standard of education among the clergy was being raised, general conditions were being improved, and it might have been hoped that better days and increased spiritual power were before this ancient Church. But the Sarajevo assassination, which shattered the peace of Europe, led also to the uprooting of the Nestorians from Kurdistan.

Turkey became involved in the Great War in November 1914, and, as with the wars between the Persian and Roman empires, between the Caliphate and the Roman Empire, and between Yaman and Najran, religious differences increased the bitterness of the struggle; Christian minorities in the Turkish Empire had a terrible ten years before them. Orthodox, Uniate, Armenian, Jacobite, and Nestorian all alike endured privation, contumely, and periodic outbursts of violence. Massacres occurred in various parts of the Turkish Empire in which hundreds of Christians were slaughtered at a time, and the total death roll must have aggregated tens of thousands. The Nestorians were in as unfortunate a position as any, because their country was in the theatre of war between the Russians and Turks. Not unnaturally, the Nestorians helped the Russians when opportunity offered, and as a community declared war on Turkey in 1915. The immediate result was a ruthless ravaging of their territory by the Turks. First they tried to take refuge in their higher mountains, but eventually they had to flee across the border to Urmi in Persia, where a Russian garrison was in control. But the Urmi region afforded them sanctuary for only a short time, for soon after the Revolution of 1917 the Russians had to leave both Turkey and Persia, and by 1918 were in final retreat. A period of great hardship followed for the Nestorians, during which, as already mentioned, they suffered the loss of their patriarch, Mar (Benjamin)[1] Shimun XIX, who was murdered by a Turk, Ismail Agha Shekak, on March 16th, 1918. He was succeeded by his younger brother, Mar (Paul)[2] Shimun XX. As it became clear that it was unsafe to remain any longer in Persia, the Nestorians undertook a desperate trek to join with the British force in Mesopotamia.

For meanwhile the British advance up the Tigris valley had been progressing, though with depressing slowness. By September 1915 General Townshend had captured Kut al Imara. He was able to continue his

[1] Benyamin.   [2] Polus.

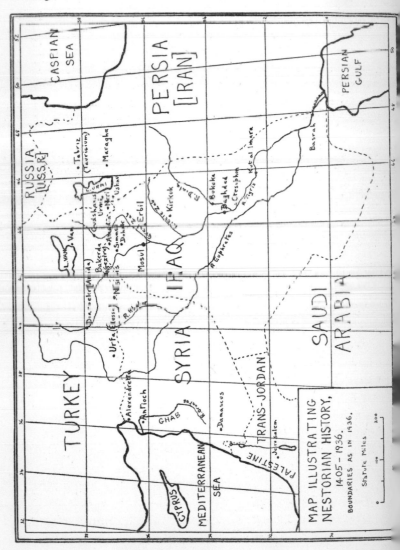

MAP ILLUSTRATING
NESTORIAN HISTORY,
1405-1936.
BOUNDARIES AS IN 1936.

advance as far as Ctesiphon, but owing to shortage of men and supplies he had to fall back again on Kut. There he was cut off, and after an ineffective attempt by General Gorringe to break through with relief, Kut had to surrender on December 29th, 1915. In December 1916, however, General Maude, with better resources, began the advance again. By the end of February 1917 he had recaptured Kut, and Ctesiphon by the beginning of March. He went straight on to Baghdad, which he captured on March 11th. General Maude established himself for the summer at Baghdad, planning his advance for the autumn, the next great objective being Mosul. That advance was commenced in September 1917, but unfortunately General Maude succumbed to cholera on November 10th. Sir William Raine Marshall succeeded him, but the change in command inevitably meant a retardation of progress, and Marshall was not able to get beyond Kirkuk (the ancient Karkha in Garamæa) before the next summer was upon him. His difficulties were increased by the fact that more troops were available for the Turks now that the Russians had been finally routed in Kurdistan and Transcaucasia. Nevertheless, Marshall began his advance on Mosul in October 1918. The advance was conducted with masterly strategy, one section of his force going by way of Kirkuk and a more mobile section following the Tigris. The Turks had to fall rapidly back, and Mosul was captured just before the Armistice was signed.

It was this British campaign in Mesopotamia which made escape possible for the Nestorians. They set out from the Urmi region to make for the British lines, which they knew were by then (1918) beyond Baghdad. It was a terrible journey for the little community to make, for it had to be made by the women and children as well as by the men, and they had to take also their livestock and scanty possessions. They were constantly harassed by warlike tribesmen along their route, and shortage of food and water caused grave hardship. It is estimated that by the time they left Urmi they had been reduced from the pre-war 100,000 to about 70,000, and that of these not more than 50,000 arrived in Mesopotamia. Those figures are themselves eloquent of their privations and sufferings.

When they at last reached the British, a camp was established for them at Bakuba on the River Diala, about 33 miles north-east of Baghdad. Even after the Armistice, conditions for Christians in Turkey continued to be intolerable, largely because its internal state was so uncertain and unstable, and it soon became evident that there was no immediate hope of resettling the Nestorians, or the Assyrians as they are now generally called,[1] in the Hakkiari mountains of Kurdistan. It thus came about that for the time being they had to settle as refugees in Iraq. (Iraq was the

[1] See p. 179. Now that the Nestorians have developed from a melet into a virtually separate little nation, there is still more to be said for reviving some such distinctive name as Assyrian, to indicate that the bond of the community is social and racial as well as religious. The term has in fact been adopted to such an extent that references to them in *The Times*, *Hansard*, *Keesing's Contemporary Archives*, *Headway*, *Great Britain and the East* and other current literature must be looked for under the heading 'Assyrian' rather than 'Nestorian.' The present patriarch has no objection to either name.

name given to that part of the Tigris-Euphrates area
which was detached from the Turkish Empire and
made into a separate State.) At this time Iraq was
under British control, and the Assyrians were mostly
settled in the neighbourhoods of Mosul and Kirkuk.
Owing to the privations and difficulties of the march
from Urmi, and to the hardships of the first months in
Iraq, the health of the young patriarch had become
undermined, and he died in May 1920, being only
about thirty years old. He was succeeded by the
present Mar (Jesse)[1] Shimun XXI, who was consecrated on June 20th, 1920, when not quite thirteen
years old. He is reckoned as 119th in the episcopal
succession of Seleucia-Ctesiphon. At about the same
time (1919) the aged matran, Mar Isaac Hananyeshu,
died, and was succeeded by his nephew, Mar Joseph
Hananyeshu, who was then thirty-two.

For over twelve years after the war Iraq was a
mandated territory under British control, and unwit-
tingly a course of action was pursued which created a
most undesirable tension between the Assyrians and the
inhabitants of Iraq. The Assyrian men were enrolled
in various British forces, and thus became identified by
the Muslim Arabs of Iraq with both Christianity and
foreign control. In such circumstances, and in such
unsettled times, it was inevitable that incidents would
occur which would not soon be forgotten. Thus at a
brawl at Kirkuk in 1924, Assyrian soldiery killed a
hundred Muslims. The ill-feeling between the natives

[1] Issai, Ishai, Eshai. Of these transliterations Mar Shimun personally prefers the form Eshai, as may be seen in his signature (in English
and Syriac) to the Foreword of this book.

of Iraq and the Assyrian refugees made it evident that
when the mandate expired and Iraq became an
autonomous State it would be unwise to leave these
Nestorian Christians there. All kinds of plans were
considered, but in every case there were difficulties.
Thus settlement in Persia was mooted; or in Brazil; or
in British Guiana. But in each case there were insuper-
able objections. Resettlement in Kurdistan was also
discussed, perhaps giving them independence as a
little Christian State; but it was soon realized that any
such idea was quite out of the question. Finally, it was
generally agreed that the best solution would be settlement in Syria, which was under French mandate and
seemed likely to remain so.

Still, little was actually done. The time for expiry of
the Iraq mandate drew nearer, and the Assyrians
began to consider they were being badly treated. So
many false hopes had been raised that they became
suspicious of the honesty of intention of Britain and
the League of Nations. As one of them said to an
English missionary in Mosul, 'Do you think we believe
anything you say?'[1] Unfortunately, faction also developed among themselves, and only about half of them
were satisfied with the leadership of Mar Shimun XXI.
He, no doubt, was doing the best he could for his
people, but he was very young for such responsibilities,
even by 1933 being only twenty-six. But there were
some who thought he was not insistent enough in his
demands. It is not probable that a stronger leader
could have accomplished much more, because the

1 Quoted in The Times, July 25th, 1935.

British authorities were as helpful to Mar Shimun as they could be, and for a time he was at Canterbury receiving both shelter and education under the immediate superintendence of the Archbishop of Canterbury (the late Dr. Davidson). For the principal obstacle to settlement in Syria was not policy, but finance. The Iraq government promised £125,000 toward the cost, but that would not nearly cover the total. The British government could not see its way to accepting the full responsibility, and the League of Nations evidently had no fund to draw on for such a purpose.

Most regrettably, the matter was not settled so soon as it should have been, and as the end of the mandate drew nearer tension increased. Much trouble was caused by an Assyrian extremist party headed by Yacu, and matters came to a head when in August 1933 the Muslims massacred six hundred Assyrians in the villages of Dohuk and Simmel, just north of Mosul. When such a state of tension has developed, blame is not easily apportioned; and though the British public naturally sympathized with the Assyrians, there may have been provocation. Ata Amin, chargé d'affaires at the Iraqi legation in London, in a letter to *The Times* of July 20th, 1935, refers back to this massacre, and urges that fair consideration should be given to the Arab point of view. Be that as it may, Britain had certainly been unwise in using the Nestorian Christian minority as her agents for restoring order in a Muslim country. Alternatively, as she had done so, she should have accepted definite responsibility for their future. Mr. L. S. Amery, Secretary for the Colonies, wrote a strong letter to *The Times* to that effect on July 18th, 1935 – commendable, but a little belated.

At the time of the Simmel massacre the Iraqi government decided to expel the patriarch, presumably hoping to demoralize the Assyrians by removing their natural leader. As Iraq was still under the mandate, the British Embassy had to give consent before this could be done. The consent was given, possibly under the impression that the patriarch's life would be endangered if he remained in Iraq. Accordingly, on August 10th, 1933, Mar Shimun XXI left Baghdad in a British Royal Air Force aeroplane, and was taken to Cyprus via Palestine. In October he was allowed to proceed to Geneva to plead his people's cause before the League of Nations. Since 1933 he has not been allowed to return to Iraq, and has spent his time in Geneva, Paris, London, and elsewhere, doing what he can to help his people. But for diplomatic reasons his freedom of activity has to be considerably circum-scribed, and while the European nations are so anxiously concerned about their own problems it is unlikely that the Assyrian question will receive the attention it merits.

However, the 1933 massacre certainly drew atten-tion to the urgency of the matter, and the correspond-ence columns of *The Times* reflected the fact that British public opinion was disturbed. Lord Hugh Cecil wrote saying that he had hoped the Assyrians would have settled happily in Iraq; but others with experience of the actual conditions replied expressing their convic-tion that no such hope was practical. It was generally

recognized that settlement elsewhere was the only
solution, and a Committee of the League Council was
appointed to attend to the subject. Plans for settlement
in Syria then began to be advanced a little more
rapidly, and small detachments were drafted across
the border. Arrangements were made to settle them
temporarily in the Khabur valley, with hopes that they
might eventually be transferred to the Ghab region,
the Orontes valley, which was said to be a very suitable
region for their permanent habitation. By the time
that the independence of Iraq was symbolized by the
accession of King Ghazi I on September 8th, 1933,
quite a number of Assyrians had taken up their abode
in the Khabur valley. Altogether about 4,000[1] settled
there, and it was possible to close the camp at Mosul
which had to be established after the Dohuk and
Simmel massacres; for after that disaster the Assyrians
were afraid to continue living in scattered villages. It
was hoped that the Ghab region would provide a home
for the remaining thirty or forty thousand, and that
when those in the Khabur valley were transplanted
there also, they would soon become a settled and
unified community.

But when the League of Nations Committee started
to work out the details of the scheme, unexpected
difficulties began to arise. It was found that the
scheme would cost far more than had been supposed.
Much of the Ghab region was marsh land, which would
need draining; reservoirs would have to be made; the
Orontes would have to be deepened; public offices

[1] The number has since risen to 8,500.

and other buildings would have to be erected. It was
finally estimated that the settlement would cost at
least £1,146,000. An effort was made to raise this
amount. The Iraq government promised to be responsible for £250,000 instead of £125,000, the British
government promised £250,000, the French government £380,000, and the League of Nations £86,000.
These offers left an additional £186,000 to be raised
if the scheme was to be completed. Early in April
1936 a national appeal fund was inaugurated at the
Mansion House, London, to endeavour to raise Britain's
share of this additional capital. The Lord Mayor
presided, and among those urging that the fund should
be supported were the Archbishop of Canterbury (Dr.
Cosmo Lang), Sir Samuel Hoare (former Foreign
Secretary), Mr. Anthony Eden (Foreign Secretary),
and Mr. L. S. Amery (Colonial Secretary).

But this appeal had hardly been launched when
further grave difficulties arose. It was felt that the
cost of the settlement was out of all proportion to its
advantages, and it began to be doubted whether the
region was so desirable as had been supposed. It was
discovered that the Syrian authorities contemplated
recovering 100,000 acres, but only 37,500 of these
would go to the Assyrians; it was represented that the
Arabs already in the region were unfavourably disposed
toward any such settlement; and France intimated
that her mandate would in all probability be termin-
ated within three or four years. For these reasons, on
July 5th, 1936, the Council of the League of Nations
decided that the Ghab settlement plan must be

abandoned. This was a grave disappointment to those who had been so anxious to see this scheme succeed. On July 28th, the Archbishop of Canterbury raised the matter in the House of Lords, and inquired whether settlement in some part of the British Empire might not be reconsidered. Lord Stanhope, on behalf of the government, said that the problem was not being overlooked, but added that settlement in a tropical or sub-tropical region would be unsuitable for the Assyrians, who had been used to the Kurdistan highlands.

Meanwhile, time had been blunting some of the sharp feeling which had arisen between Assyrians and Iraqi Arabs in the earlier post-war years, and hope revived that they might yet settle in Iraq. On November 16th, 1936, Mr. Anthony Eden was able to report to the House of Commons that 8,500 Assyrians were then in the upper part of the Khabur valley in Syria, but that the majority, who were still in Iraq, seemed to show signs of being willing to settle there finally, and that he thought the problem was moving towards its own settlement. This hope was reaffirmed a few weeks later (December 7th, 1936), when, in reply to a question from Colonel Wedgwood, Mr. Eden said: 'The Iraqi government have formally declared that it is their intention to ensure the welfare and protection of all minorities in Iraq, and such information as I have received shows that this declaration is being fully carried out.'

While this may be true, the fact remains that the patriarch is still unable to return to his people, to take up his rightful position as spiritual leader and head of

the melet.   Recently he graciously granted the present
writer an interview in London,[1] and although he
speaks with deliberate caution, it is clear that he does
not think settlement in Iraq provides a final solution.
He still hopes that it will be possible for his people to
be provided with a territory where they may live in
peace and confidence.   After all, there are only about
30,000 of them (apart from some in south Russia,
whose fortunes seem to have diverged from those of the
main sections), so the problem should not be impossibly
formidable.   Of these 30,000, Mar Shimun estimates
that about 22,000 are in Iraq and 8,500 in Syria, in
the Khabur valley.   Those in Iraq live mostly in and
around Baghdad and Mosul, while some are in the
regions of Kirkuk and Erbil.   In the absence of the
patriarch, they are led by the matran, Mar Joseph
Hananyeshu, who resides at Harir, near Erbil.   Beside
the matran, there is only one other bishop, so that the
Nestorian episcopate now comprises only the patriarch,
Mar (Jesse)[2] Shimun XXI; two metropolitans, Mar
Joseph Hananyeshu and Mar Timotheus (see p. 163);
and one bishop.

Here, then, hopeful for a brighter future, we must
leave the Nestorian Church, the twentieth century
Assyrians, a remnant some thirty thousand strong which
in our own time has endured hardships as great as any
in its history.   It may yet be that we shall see them
happily resettled in the localities where their historic
Church gained its primal strength, and that Baghdad,
Mosul, and Kirkuk may once again become centres of

[1] February 13th, 1937.   [2] Eshai.

Nestorian Christianity. If these hopes are fulfilled, they may revive again to some measure of strength and prosperity; and even if their patriarch will never again be the head of a great Church stretching right across Asia, he may at least be the respected head of an autocephalous Christian Church in Iraq, justly proud of its long history, yet not unwilling to accept help and counsel from their Christian brethren of the West. Alternatively, perhaps even preferably, it may be that the patriarch's hopes will be fulfilled, and that a home will be provided for them in a land where they will be free to work out their destiny according to their own faith and culture. No one who knows their history would deny that this is their due.

Apart from such hopes, which at their best fulfilment could reproduce no more than a meagre vestige of the extent and power of the medieval Nestorian Church, is there nothing to show as the result of this Church's long and chequered history, nothing but a reduced minority in Iraq? In reply to such a question two things may be said:

First, that no cross-section made in time gives data for valuations in terms of eternity. Our imagination must visualize the whole company of Christians brought into the fold of Christ during the course of the centuries. If the Christian faith is true, the total Nestorian Church is not a remnant in Iraq: it is a great multitude, including in its numbers martyrs and missionaries who gave their all for Christ; a great company of Christians who, even though on earth attached to a Church not in communion with the rest of Christendom, will none the less be surely accorded their place in the Church Triumphant.

Second, and finally, the fact that this Church has survived at all gives courage and example to modern Christians. From the very start the Nestorian Christians have always been a minority in lands of other faiths; throughout their history they have been subject to persecution and oppression; there has never been a time, except for a while under the ilkhans, when it would not have profited them to renounce their faith. Such steadfastness is an example for all time, and an eternal testimony to the glory of a faith for the sake of which all else is counted well lost.

BIBLIOGRAPHY

ADENEY, W. F.: *Greek and Eastern Churches.*

AMANN, ABBÉ: *The Church of the Early Centuries.*

ARNOLD, T.: *The Preaching of Islam.*

ASSEMANI, J. S.: *Bibliotheca Orientalis.*

BADGER, G. P.: *The Nestorians and their Rituals.*

BARTLET, J. V., & CARLYLE, A. J.: *Christianity in History.*

BETHUNE-BAKER, J. F.: *Introduction to the Early History of Christian Doctrine.*

BETHUNE-BAKER, J. F.: *Nestorius and his Teaching.*

BROWNE, E. G.: *Literary History of Persia.*

BROWNE, L. E.: *The Eclipse of Christianity in Asia.*

Bulletin of the John Rylands Library (Manchester): articles by Dr. A. Mingana in Vols. IX.–XI.

BURKITT, F. C.: *Early Christianity outside the Roman Empire.*

Cambridge Medieval History.

CHABOT: *Histoire de Jab-Alaha, Patriarche, et de Raban Sauma.*

CHEIKHO, L.: *Le Christianisme et la littérature chrétienne en Arabie avant l'Islam.*

CHWOLSON: see *Mémoires de l'Académie Impériale de Sciences de St Pétersbourg.*

CLAVIJO: *Embassy to Tamerlane.* (English translation by Guy Le Strange.)

COSMAS INDICOPLEUSTES: *Topographia Christiana.* (In Migne, *Patrologia Græca*, LXXXVIII.)

COWPER, B. H.: *Syriac Grammar.*

Encyclopædia Britannica: relevant articles (fourteenth edition unless otherwise stated).

Encyclopædia of Religion and Ethics (editor, J. Hastings): relevant articles.

FOAKES-JACKSON, F. J.: *History of the Christian Church to A.D. 461.*

FORTESCUE, ADRIAN: *Lesser Eastern Churches.*

FORTESCUE, ADRIAN: *Uniate Eastern Churches.*

GIESELER, J. C. L.: *Compendium of Ecclesiastical History.* (English translation by Samuel Davidson.)

HARNACK, ADOLF: *The Expansion of Christianity in the First Three Centuries.* (English translation by James Moffatt.)

HOWORTH, H. H.: *History of the Mongols.*

HUC: *Christianity in China.*

KIDD, B. J.: *Churches of Eastern Christendom.*

LABOURT, J.: *De Timotheo I Nestorianorum Patriarcha et Christianorum condicione sub Caliphis.*

LABOURT, J.: *Le Christianisme dans l'empire perse.*

LEAGUE OF NATIONS UNION: *Refugees and the League.* (Author not named.)

LE QUIEN: *Oriens Christianus.*

LOOFS, FRIEDRICH: *Nestoriana.*

LOOFS, FRIEDRICH: *Nestorius.*

MACARTNEY, C. A.: *Refugees.*

MACKINTOSH, H. R.: *The Person of Jesus Christ.*

MACLEAN & BROWNE: *The Catholicos of the East.*

MARGA, THOMAS OF: *Historia Monastica.* (In W. Budge, *The Book of Governors.*)

Mémoires de l'Académie Impériale de Sciences de St. Pétersbourg: articles by Chwolson in Vols. XXXIV. and XXXVII.

MINGANA, A.: see *Bulletin of the John Rylands Library.*

MOBERG, A.: *The Book of the Himyarites.*

MUIR, WILLIAM: *The Coran, its Composition and Teaching.*

NAU, F.: *L'expansion Nestorienne en Asie.*

NEALE: *History of the Holy Eastern Church.*

NESTORIUS: *The Bazaar of Heraclides.* (Editions by P. F. Bedjan (German), F. Nau (French), and Driver & Hodgson (English).)

PALMER, E. H.: *Arabic Grammar.* (In Trübner's series.)

PALMER, E. H.: *The Quran.* (Translation, being Vols. VI. and IX. of *Sacred Books of the East.*)

PRICE: *History of Muhammadanism.*

RAVEN, C. E.: *Apollinarianism.*

ROBINSON, C. H.: *History of Christian Missions.*

RODWELL, J. M.: *The Koran.* (Translation.)

STAFFORD, COLONEL: *The Tragedy of the Assyrians.*

STANLEY, A. P.: *The Eastern Church.*

STEWART, JOHN: *Nestorian Missionary Enterprise.*

The Assyrian Tragedy. (Author not named. Only mark 'Imp. Granchamp, Annemasse.')

TOZER, H. F.: *The Church and the Eastern Empire.*

WIGRAM, W. A.: *History of the Assyrian Church.*

WILTSCH, J. E. T.: *Handbook of the Geography and Statistics of the Church.* (English translation by John Leitch.)

YULE, H.: *Cathay and the Way Thither.*

ZWEMER, S.: *Islam.*

INDEX

(The positions of places marked on the maps are given to the nearest degree, together with the page numbers of the maps on which they appear.)

Manichæans, 62, 93
  note on, 93
Mansur, 93, 102, 104
Maota, 127
Maps, list of, 20
Mar, Syriac title of respect,
  'Lord,' 98
  derivatives, Mari, 'My Lord,'
  Mart, 'Lady'
Mar Aba I, 65, 71–72
  conversion of, 71
Maragha (37 N. 46 E.: 121, 122,
  136, 196), 118, 124, 155, 159,
  170
  monastery at, 155
Marangerd, 75, 115
Mar Babai the Great, 67, 74–75
Marcian, 40
Mardin, 54
  And see Mardis
Mardis (mod. Mardin), (37 N.
  41 E.: 121, 122), 114, 123,
  159
Marga. *See* Maragha
Mar Hananyeshu (Isaac), 185,
  187, 199
Mar Hananyeshu (Joseph), 199,
  206
Mari, 97–100
Maris, 38, 117, 152
  Ibas' letter to, 38
Markabta, synod at, 48, 54
Maronites, 109
Marshall, Sir W. R., 197
Mar Shimun XII, 173
Mar Shimun XIII, 173
Mar Shimun XVIII (Reuben),
  185
Mar Shimun XIX (Benjamin),
  185, 195
Mar Shimun XX (Paul), 195, 199
Mar Shimun XXI (Jesse, Eshai),
  7, 199–200, 202, 205–206
Mar Timotheus (of India), 163,
  206
Mart Maryam ('Lady Mary'), 97,
  190
Marutha, 48
Marwan I, 139
Marwan II, 140

Masalians, 109
Masamig, island of, 116, 124
Masruq, 76–77
Mathota, 59
Matran, 184–185, 199
Maude, General, 197
Maurice, 66
Mawardi, 99–100
Maximian, 32
Mecca (21 N. 40 E.. 38), 77–78,
  84
Medina (25 N. 40 E.: 58), 60, 78.
  84
Melet (millah, millet), 47, 88–89,
  92, 97, 99, 146, 176
Melkites, 106
Memnon of Ephesus, 31–32
Merkites (55 N. 115 E.: 136), 128
Merv (38 N. 62 E.: 58, 121, 136),
  57, 69, 84, 91, 117, 124, 141,
  143
Mesopotamia, 176, 195–198
Metropolitans, place of in hier-
  archy, 46, 55
Metropolitan provinces, lists of,
  57, 112–124
Metropolitan system, development
  of, 110
Mllapur, 79, 161–162
Ming dynasty, 168
Missions to the Nestorians, mo-
  dern, 177–182
Mohammed, -an, -ism. *See* Mu-
  hammad, -an, -ism
Monasteries, monasticism, 59, 73–
  74, 131, 133–135, 155
Mongolia, 143, 145
Mongols, 111, 128–130, 140–150,
  153–154, 164, 166, 168
  expansion, 84, 111, 113
  terror caused by, 142–144
  persecutions by. *See* Persecu-
  tions, Mongol
Monophysitism, 25, 51, 54, 75,
  126
  definition of, 40
Monothelites, 109
Mopsuestia (37 N. 36 E.: 121), 126
  And see Theodore of Mopsuestia
Moslem. *See* Muslim

SUPPLEMENTAL INDEX OF VARIANTS IN THE SPELLING OF NAMES

Where variants are given without comment, the first form is that which will be found in the general index. 'anc.' and 'mod.' will be used to indicate ancient and modern forms respectively. Many names have easily recognized English, Latin, and Greek forms, such as Timothy, Timotheus, Timotheos; Gregory, Gregorius, Gregorios. These will not usually be listed, nor will easily recognizable Latinized forms of oriental names, such as Abdalmalecus for Abdalmalik.

Abagha, Abaga, Abaka
Abdishu, Abdiso. *See* Ebedyeshu
Abul Faraj, Aboul Faradj, Abul-pharagius
Acacius, Akak
Acbara. *See* Ochara
Acre, Akka, Accho, Acco, St. Jean d'Acre, Ptolemais
Adorbigana, Adharbaijan. *See* Atropatene
Ahai, Achæus
Al-, the Arabic article
(For names beginning with this, hyphened or directly joined *see without this prefix.*)
Alamundar. *See* Mundhar
Aleppo. *See* Berrhoea
Al-Madaïn. *See* Madaïn
Almansor. *See* Mansur
Al-Mundhar. *See* Mundhar
Alopen, Alopu, Olopun, Olopwen
Amadia, Amadiyah
Amida, Amid, mod. Diarbekr, q.v.
Amrus, Amr
Ananjesu. *See* Hananyeshu
Anbar, Anbara, Enbar, el-Anbar
Arbela, Arbil. *See* Erbil
Ardashir (person), Artaxerxes
Ardashir (place). *See* Seleucia
Arghun, Argon
Aria. *See* Herat

Atropatene, Adorbigana, Athro-patakan, Adharbaijan, Azer-badegan, mod. Azerbaijan, Aderbijan

Babai, Babhai, Babwai, Babæus, bishop of Seleucia-Ctesiphon, 497–502
Babowai, Babwai, Babai, Ba-buæus, Babæus, bishop of Seleu-cia-Ctesiphon, 457–484
(There is considerable confusion between these two sets of names, some considering them different, others considering them the same. Those who consider them the same name distinguish them as Babwai, Babai, Babæus II and I respectively.)
Barbasemin, Bar Bashmin, Bar-basemen, Barbaseminus
Baghdad, Bagdad
Bajarmai, Beth Garma, Beth Garmai. *See* Garamæa
Bakerda, Beth Zabda, Gezira, Gozarta, mod. Jezireh
Barsumas, Bar Sauma
Basrah, Basra, Bassora, Bassara, Busra
Berrhoea, Beroca, Berea, Beria, Chalybon-Beroea, Khalep-Beroea, Khalep, Halep, mod. Aleppo, Haleb, Halab.

223